U.S. Border Patrol

The Journey

& the Solution to the Illegal Alien Problem

By Donald R. Coppock

Chief, U.S. Border Patrol, Retired

NEW FORUMS

Stillwater, Oklahoma
U.S.A.

NEW FORUMS PRESS

Published in the United States of America
by New Forums Press, 1018 S. Lewis St.
Stillwater, OK 74074
Phone: 405-372-6158

Library of Congress Cataloging-in-Publication Data Pending

This book may be ordered in bulk quantities at a discount by calling 1-800-
606-3766. Printed in the United States of America.

ISBN 10: 1-58107-147-7

Contents

For the loves of my life,
my wife Shirley and our daughter Mary-Blue.
Our Grandchildren
Mary Elizabeth, Donald, Virginia-Blue
and our capable and beloved son-in-law
John Ster.

Foreword

When speaking of the United States Border Patrol, one must include Donald R. Coppock. I have known Mr. Coppock for over 45 years and he is the epitome of what the Border Patrol stands for – courage, honor, and dedication. He has always been a leader by example and will never compromise his principles or integrity for personal gain. He proudly displays his love of God, Country and the Patrol.

We are living in a period of history when our nation faces great responsibilities and challenges in protecting our shores. The U.S. Border Patrol has shared in these responsibilities, past, present and, undoubtedly, the future.

In this book, Don tells the inside story of his many years with the patrol. His collective thoughts and information give a powerful account of the patrol from 1941 to 1973. This book packs both a historical and personal punch.....he captures the esprit-de-corps of the patrol with actual accounts as experienced by him.

I highly recommend this book to anyone wanting a factual record of the Border Patrol in action and a piece of history little known to the majority of the public. It is an exciting experience to journey with Don down through the years as he recalls one of the most storied periods relating to the patrol. You will also gain an insight to one of the most notable Border Patrol officers I have ever known.

Buck Brandemuehl
Chief of the Border Patrol, Retired

Preface

Donald R. Coppock was born December 8, 1910, and was age 95 when he started to write *The Journey.* If only I could package and sell his work ethic, stamina and determination, I would be financially well off. I'm already rich just by having him as my friend.

I first met Don in 1951 when I entered on duty with the United States Border Patrol at El Paso. He was already a ten year Patrol veteran on the first rung of his career ladder that took him all the way to the top. Our country was divided into 23 Border Patrol Sectors. He was one of several Senior Patrol Inspectors then in the El Paso Sector, and he retired more than 20 years later from Washington with the title of CHIEF OF THE UNITED STATES BORDER PATROL. His book is a colorful recounting of his life and career.

Don and I never worked a single duty shift together, but had brief encounters along the way as our divergent careers put us on the same plane from time to time. For instance, I was one of those he led on the 1954 Wetback Drive when we removed 1.4 million illegal aliens from the United States. I left home on May 15th and began a "two week assignment" that lasted until December 20th.

I was in charge of the Dallas Immigration Office in 1973 when we were responsible for the entire state of Oklahoma and 126 counties in Texas. In June of that year, Don called and asked me to meet his plane. He was returning from an inspection trip in the lower Rio

Grande Valley and had a layover in Dallas. It was Friday. We retrieved his bag and I drove him to the hotel where we talked business for a couple of hours. We had breakfast on Saturday and I put him on the plane to Washington. Early on Monday, I learned that Don had announced his retirement from 32 years in the United States Border Patrol. We had talked about many things during his layover in Dallas, but *retirement* was not among them. He had played his cards close to his chest right to the very end.

When I retired I immediately joined the Fraternal Order of Retired Border Patrol Officers and through it we really became friends. Don was one of the founders and a real powerhouse. In 1984 he persuaded me to join the Border Patrol Museum Board of Trustees also, and our relationship continues to grow stronger each day. He still "plays them close to his chest", but he holds nothing back in this book.

During his tenure as Chief of the United States Border Patrol, unique ancillary assignments led him to friendships and/or close personal relationships with numerous high ranking labor, military, political, religious, judicial and government officials at a time of social unrest in this country. After retirement, he worked on the Nixon impeachment committee, followed by several years with the Legal Services Corporation. He is uniquely qualified to write such an insightful book.

Walter V. Edwards
Associate Regional Commissioner
Enforcement, Retired

Acknowledgments

I want to thank my wife, Shirley, and others who encouraged me to write this book. During my career we lived in 25 houses and apartments. Shirley and my daughter, Mary-Blue, never complained about the moves but were always helpful and supportive. I want to thank my son-in-law, John Ster, who was helpful, and I could not of chosen a nicer son-in-law if I had done the choosing myself. I probably wouldn't of written this book if it hadn't been for Deborah Cunningham who located boxes of files, dug the files out of the boxes and arranged then in chronological order. After the Border Patrol Museum was first opened, Buck Brandemuehl and Walt Edwards flew with me to El Paso numerous times to put out fires and they helped tremendously to make the Border Patrol Museum become a reality and a National treasure that will be appreciated and enjoyed by generations to come. Many of my comments relating to my paternal Grandparents were taken from a book entitled *The Lives and Times of Alvin and Laura Coppock*, written by a cousin, Sheldon Jackson. I also want to thank Keshia Cunningham who helped with the editing of the book.

Chapter One

The Early Years

Over the years my family and others have urged me to write about my observations and extraordinary experiences while serving in the U.S. Border Patrol. Until now I have refused to write about my experiences because of the discipline, work and research it would take. But after repetitious requests, I finally agreed that I would make an effort. In order to make this history complete I need to write about the early days, which provide the background for this story.

My paternal grandparents were Alvin and Laura Coppock. At the time of the land run into the Cherokee Outlet/Strip that occurred on September 16, 1893, they were residing near Weber, Kansas, in Jewel County that bordered the Nebraska state line. That year Alvin staked a claim on a quarter section of land $3^{1/3}$ miles northeast of what is now Cherokee, Oklahoma. It was to become the Coppock homestead. Alvin returned to Weber, Kansas, and prepared for the move to the family's new home in the Oklahoma Territory. On March 1, 1894, he held a sale to sell his farm equipment and other items that he could not move. On March 3, they departed for their new home. Their "moving vans" were two large covered wagons. The first wagon held their bedding, foods, personal items, and was also where most of their nine children rode. The second wagon contained a few pieces of furniture, farm tools, a stove, kitchen utensils, a few chickens and food for the livestock. Grandfather drove the first wagon, his eldest son Chester drove the second wagon, and the second oldest son, Stanley, age 13, rode horseback and drove their horses and the cows, which they milked each morning and evening.

On the ninth evening they camped just north of the Salt Fork of the Arkansas River, a short distance from their destination. Very early on Sunday, March 11, 1894, they broke camp, forded the river, and within an hour they arrived at the home of William Howard, a friend who had moved down from Kansas the year before. There was a happy reunion with their loved ones. They had been neighbors in Kansas, and Mrs. Howard was my grandmothers' sister. The Howards placed planks on boxes and chairs so all of them would be able to sit for Sunday school and Quaker services. With the Coppock's nine children and the Howard's 12, there were enough to almost fill a church.

The first "need" to face the Coppocks was having a place to live. As they camped on their quarter section of land, they planned the location of their home and farm buildings. They would need to have a cistern, as the well water was too salty to drink. Before the end of the first week, Grandfather Alvin took his largest wagon on a two-day trip to Kiowa, Kansas, some 25 miles away, to purchase lumber for their new house. With the help of the Howards, they constructed a two-story, five room wood house that was the Coppock home. When that was completed, they went to work on an adjoining sod house that would be their kitchen and dining room for many years. They were now settled in their "promised land."

The settlers found that living in the Cherokee Strip had its hardships, but it was never boring. I recall my father, Murray Coppock, telling me about breaking out the land. They used a sod plow pulled by a team of horses. While plowing the sod, they killed so many rattlesnakes that they filled a gallon can with snake rattles. It was fortunate for the Quaker settlers that their faith was strong, as their first three years in the Strip, 1894 through 1896, tested their mettle. They had arrived in the strip at the beginning of a drought such as they had never seen. But finally, the rains came. In the fall of 1896 they sowed winter wheat. It all came up which provided their livestock with a good winter wheat pasture. The crop was so good, some claimed 40 bushels to the acre, and the price reached $1 per bushel.

My paternal grandparents fervently believed in education; they also strongly encouraged spreading the word of God. They and their neighbors constructed a 30-by-40-foot sod building that would be used as the settler's first grade school and the Friends Church. The school opened in the fall of 1894, with Stella Howard serving as the first teacher.

The community now needed a high school. In February 1895, a year after the elementary school was constructed, a decision was made to circulate a subscription to determine how much money could be raised toward the construction of a Friends academy/high school building. Times were hard and pledges represented a real sacrifice. In spite of conditions, Alvin Coppock made a substantial pledge toward the cost of the building, which was estimated at $600. After all the planning was completed, increasing costs made it appear that they would not be able to go through with the project. At this time, Alvin Coppock made an additional pledge of $350, an enormous amount of money in those days. In view of this pledge, the project was given new life. Construction began on a two-story frame structure, 28 by 48 feet, divided below into an auditorium, reception and library rooms, and the above floor was divided into five rooms for a girl's dormitory. The first high school in the area opened in the fall of 1897. The Friends Church moved from the sod building to the Academy upon its completion.

When the high school opened, it had an enrollment of 75 students; enrollment increased to 99 students during the second year. Visiting educators such as the President of Friends University in Wichita, Kansas, and lecturers like the temperance crusader, Carrie Nation, enriched and broadened students' spiritual and moral horizons. All of Alvin and Laura's nine children graduated from the Academy. During most of the Academy's history, either Alvin or Laura served as President of the Board of Trustees. In addition, they traveled by horse and buggy to establish numerous Friends churches in the Northwest Oklahoma Territory. Alvin was also on the Board of Directors that established Friends University in Wichita, Kansas, and the Friends Bible College in Haviland, Kansas. The four living sons all had good voices, and they formed a quartet that sang at church services and social gatherings throughout the area. Additionally, they were quite successful in life. Stanley was a rancher and State Senator; Roy was elected to the State Legislature and was chairman of the State Board of Affairs; Murray, my father, was a farmer/rancher, a lecturer of the Masonic Grand Lodge of Oklahoma, and later served as its Grand Master; and, Willard was a farmer and served as Treasurer of Alfalfa County, Oklahoma, for many years. My father attended Friends University in Wichita, Kansas, and was the catcher on their baseball team. I recently found a pennant with the words "Friends University versus Fairmont College." The battery was Coppock and (I'll call him) Bill, as he has living relatives. My father told me that he was an outstanding pitcher. He later played for the St. Louis Cardinals, but he was released with the statement that he had a million dollar arm but a 10-cent head.

My mother was Mary Blue. Her father, Benjamin Franklin Blue, was the Treasurer of the small town of Ingersoll, Oklahoma. He was a farmer and he was also in the cattle business. He was in partnership with a neighbor named G. D. Azbill. They built a telephone line between their farms, and had the first telephones in the area. My mother and father met while attending Stella Academy. After they were engaged, my father built a three bedroom, two-story house on his farm, which was located some two miles northeast of Cherokee, Oklahoma. Dad and mother moved into the house the night they were married and they never moved. They were married March 3, 1910, at an evening ceremony at my maternal grandparent's home in Ingersoll, Oklahoma.

Their friends and neighbors attended the wedding and reception. As was the custom, their friends planned on shivareeing them that night. This was a practice of going to newly-weds' homes after their weddings, and beating on pans and shouting in order to disrupt any amorous endeavors. Anticipating this, my parents spent most of the night in a buggy in father's field northwest of their house. Since I was born almost nine months to the day after the wedding, I could possibly have been conceived in their buggy. I never had the nerve to ask them, so I'll never know. I recall my father saying that he lived in three townships, two counties, a territory and a state and never moved.

Chapter Two
Growing Up and Getting an Education

A t the age of 12, I was helping my father on the farm. I helped plow the land with four head of horses and helped in the milking of 8 to 12 cows, twice daily; then I separated the milk with a hand-operated separator. This work was arduous, but I believe it helped me to develop a good work ethic. It was an agricultural society, and there was no juvenile delinquency, as children were kept busy doing chores and other work. As I write about milking the cows it reminded me of an amusing story. A Quaker farmer was milking his cows when the one he was milking kept switching his tail hitting him on his face and head. He finally became quite agitated and he said to the cow; I cannot curse thee and I cannot hit thee but I can twist thy damn tail.

I have many fond memories of my childhood, and the first one that I recall was going to my maternal grandparents for Christmas dinner. The ground was covered with snow, and my father had taken the wheels off the buggy and replaced them with snow runners.

I normally walked some two miles to school, but occasionally I would get a ride on my uncle's wheat truck. He was a successful farmer, but quite thrifty.

When he bought the truck, he didn't buy a cab for it and the driver had to sit on the gas tank. One winter day my cousin Alvin drove the truck into our farm with the radiator frozen and steaming. While trying to help him, I told Alvin that the steam smelled like whisky (I don't know how I knew what whiskey smelled like at that age). He replied that it really was whiskey in the radiator. Then he told me that he always carried a shotgun behind the gas tank, and a few days before, when driving to school, a cottontail rabbit ran across the road at an intersection. He grabbed the gun, held it over his head, and ran through the grass intending to shoot the rabbit when he chased it back into the road. Instead, he stumbled over something, and when he looked to see what it was, he discovered that it was a 10-gallon barrel of whiskey. That evening he took the barrel of whiskey home, and his father used the whiskey as antifreeze in all of his vehicles.

Another of my fondest memories of my childhood was about my uncle, Meech Blue, my mother's brother. He owned two Ford agencies in Oklahoma, one in Alva and one in Cherokee, where he lived. He and another Cherokee merchant, C. H. Baker, sponsored a teen baseball team. In the spring of 1921 the Yankees and the Brooklyn Dodgers played an exhibition game in Oklahoma City. Uncle Meech took the entire baseball team to the game. Prior to moving to Cherokee, Meech had a town baseball team in Protection, Kansas. On the team was an underarm pitcher named Carl Mays who at the time of our trip was pitching for the New York, Yankees. We were able to see Babe Ruth play, and we got to meet

Carl Mays. After Mr. Mays retired, he spent the summers in Day, Oregon and the winters at his home in El Cajon, California, a suburb of San Diego. In the 1960s while on a business trip to our Chula Vista Border Patrol Sector, I read that Mr. Mays had passed away. I wrote to Mrs. Mays expressing my condolences, and related the above information to her. I received a very nice letter from her letting me know how much she appreciated hearing the story.

Another fond memory I recall was when I was 13 years of age; I accompanied my parents to Haviland, Kansas to attend my paternal grandparents' golden wedding anniversary. They were both ordained Quaker ministers, and they married themselves again, the same way they had done it 50 years earlier.

I attended Cherokee High School and, in addition to my studies, I played football, tennis and basketball. My favorite sport, by far, was basketball. After graduating from high school, I attended Northwestern State University in Alva, Oklahoma. While there, I played two years of varsity basketball. I was only able to attend college by working and by receiving financial help from an uncle, who was a very generous person. I worked for the university for 25 cents per hour maintaining the tennis courts, and I worked at the Monfort Drug Store jerking sodas.

My third year of college I was persuaded to attend and play basketball, at what is now Oklahoma State University. There was a rule at that time that in Class A universities you had to play a year of freshman ball before you could play on the varsity team. While at Oklahoma State, I got a call early one morning from Bruce Drake, the coach of the Oklahoma City semi-pro basketball team, asking me if I would play for them that night against the Wichita Henrys in Wichita, Kansas, if he came by and picked me up. He then said that he would pay me $100 and that I would play for a person named Perry McCoy who was unavailable. I told him that I didn't want to jeopardize my amateur standing so I would only take $10 for expenses. We beat the Wichita Henrys who had been national champions the year before. I might as well have taken the $100, as I played under the name of Perry McCoy, which was definitely an infraction of the rules.

I went back to Oklahoma State in the fall of 1931 before school started, as the basketball coach had promised me a job. While waiting, I received a call from the basketball coach at Northwestern State University. He informed me that he had a good job for me if I would return to Northwestern. He told me that Transcontinental Air Transport (TAT), later to become Trans World Airlines, was flying Ford tri-motored planes that would pick up passengers in Columbus, Ohio, after they arrived there by a passenger train from New York, and would fly them to Waynoka, Oklahoma. There they would have dinner in one of the Santa Fe's famed Harvey House restaurants. After dinner they boarded a train that would take them to Clovis, New Mexico, where they then would board a plane that would take them to Los Angeles, California. It was the beginning of coast-to-coast travel, taking a mere 48 hours. Charles Lindberg was the dreamer and the major owner of the company.

After 18 months of operation, the company had lost seven million dollars, as well as two airplanes with all the passengers aboard. It was the end of TAT, and it merged with Trans World Airlines. At the beginning of the school year in 1931, the airline was building an auxiliary airfield Northwest of Alva, Oklahoma, and I was hired for $6 a day to fuel two caterpillar tractors each evening and to sleep there at night. At that time $6 a day salary was considered a good wage. I immediately packed my meager belongings and hitchhiked back to Northwestern State University.

I played four years of varsity basketball at Northwestern, and I was fortunate to be selected Collegiate All State in my junior year. After graduation in 1933, I planned on teaching and coaching. Soon thereafter a friend suggested that I go to Wichita, Kansas and apply for a job with the Southern Kansas Bus Company, as they had a semi-pro basketball team and were looking for players. I went to Wichita and was hired that same day. There were no professional teams at that time, but there were semi-pro teams such as the Denver Pigs (representing the Piggly Wiggly food chain), the Tulsa Oilers, Wichita Henrys, the Southern Kansas Stage Lines, and Gridley Motors. I played the first year with the Southern Kansas Stage Lines, and the next year I was traded to the Gridley Motors. After that season ended I hung up my suit and played no more. I stayed with the Southern Kansas Stage Lines, which later became Santa Fe Trailways for seven years before I joined the U. S. Border Patrol.

Chapter Three
The Beginning of My Career in the Border Patrol

In early 1940 I read an article in the newspaper that the Border Patrol force was being increased and they were hiring new inspectors. I applied for the job and subsequently took the written examination in Wichita, Kansas, and the oral examination at the Veterans Hospital in Muskogee, Oklahoma.

On August 28, 1940, I married Shirley Sheridan, a native of Meeker, Colorado, and in 2005 we celebrated our 65th wedding anniversary. Marrying Shirley was the best thing that ever happened to me. She told me many times that her father always told her to be thankful for all you have, and she taught me gratitude, humility and generosity. Any successes that I may have achieved during our long marriage I can attribute to her.

It was also in 1940 that I received word that I had been accepted for employment in the Border Patrol, and I was told to report for duty in El Paso on February 7, 1941. The next day was a Saturday, and I worked a half-day shift with an old-timer whose name I no longer recall. On Sunday I drove to headquarters, and when I arrived there was only one officer on duty. He told me that an officer had accidentally been shot, and all the other officers were at St. Mary's Hospital. He suggested that I go to the hospital, as the officer had bled profusely, and needed a blood transfusion. When I arrived at the hospital, my blood was tested and it turned out that only the Chief's blood and mine matched that of the injured officer. Of course I was chosen, and I laid beside the officer as the transfusion was made. The transfusion apparently did not help as the officer died a few days later.

On Monday I attended the seventh session of the Border Patrol Training School, which lasted a little over a month. The session ended on a Friday, and I was scheduled to work the 4:00 p.m. to midnight shift on the following Monday. However, at about 8:30 a.m. that day there was a knock on my apartment door (we didn't yet have a telephone). It was the Assistant Chief Patrol Inspector, Bill Yeager, nattily attired in dress uniform. He informed me that the Chief wanted me to report to duty as soon as possible for a special detail. I had no idea what the detail might entail, but I imagined that there were a large number of aliens trying to enter the United States illegally. I hurriedly put on my uniform, strapped on my service revolver, and reported to the Chief, who asked me, *"Coppock, you know how to drive a truck, don't you?"* When I told him that I did, he told me to take the truck and go up the valley to the Strauss, New Mexico Station and pick up a load of baled hay; then to take it to the Sierra Blanca Horse Station which was located some eighty miles down river from El Paso. At both stations I noticed that all of the horses were thoroughbreds. When I returned to headquarters about 4:00

p.m. the shifts were changing and wanting to be one of the boys, I inquired to no one in particular why the Border Patrol was using thoroughbred horses to patrol the border. There was a long silence. Then one of the officers asked what was the matter with thoroughbreds, and what kind of horse would I like. I replied that thoroughbreds were very high strung and nervous, and that I would prefer Morgan horses, as they had a nice gate and a serene personality.

The next day when I reported for duty there was a note in my box instructing me to report to the Chief Patrol Inspector, G. J. McBee. When we met, he told me that I was being transferred to the horse station at Strauss, New Mexico. The next day I reported to my new station. Egbert Crossett was the Senior Patrol Inspector; the work was interesting; and I enjoyed the almost three years I was there. Incidentally, to prove the point I had made about the thoroughbreds, one of the horses bucked almost every time he was ridden. While at the Strauss Station, I worked with several officers, but there were 3 that became lifelong friends: Bill Turner, Roy Young, and John Ward. One day when I was still on probation and working with Bill Turner, we had cut sign along the border, and finding no tracks of aliens crossing the border and still having time left on our shift, we decided to observe traffic at what was called the "crossroads", where Mesa Avenue and Highway 80 merged north of El Paso. Shortly thereafter, we observed a car with a Mexican license plate traveling north. We stopped the car, and the passenger in the vehicle was General Quinones, who was in charge of the army post in Juarez, Mexico. He presented a local crossing card, and although local cardholders were restricted to the city limits of El Paso, we were cautious. We asked the General to follow us four miles up the road to Canutillo, Texas, which was where we called headquarters for advice. Being a Sunday, there were no supervisors on duty, but a veteran officer stated that he thought we should let the General and his driver proceed on their trip, which we did. The next day Mr. Crossett told Bill and me that he had been instructed to bring us to the District Director's Office at 9:00 a.m. the next day. Crossett picked us up, and on the way to El Paso he said that he didn't know what the District Director wanted to see us about. *"But, whatever it is,"* he said, *"I'll support you."* He then said it was probably about us stopping and questioning General Quinones, and then he said, *"If it is, you tell the District Director that I didn't assign you to observe traffic."* Some support! When we met with the District Director he was very nice, asking us how long we had detained the General. We told him that it hadn't been over twenty minutes at the most, and he replied that it had been reported to him that we had detained the General anywhere from an hour to half a day. He then said that when we encountered a person with the stature of the General, to pat him on the back and tell him to have a good trip.

Another incident also involved Bill Turner. We had been cutting sign along the border on horseback, and when we arrived back at the corrals, we unsaddled the horses, fed them, and got back in the truck. Bill, an outstanding pistol shooter, was sitting in the passenger seat, and he told me that he had lightened the trigger on his service revolver and he wanted me to try it. He unloaded the revolver, handed it to me, and asked me to try the trigger pull. After trying it a few times, I handed it back to him and he reloaded the revolver. He then absentmindedly pulled the hammer back and pulled the trigger, making a direct hit on the radio. As I recall, Bill wasn't reprimanded, but he was required to pay for a new radio.

In yet another weapons incident, an officer named Cochinar (I don't recall his first name) was in the barn getting hay to feed the horses, when he saw a rat running along a rafter. He took out his revolver and tried to shoot the rat; he missed the rat and the bullet went through the barn wall and killed a horse. I don't recall how this incident was resolved, but it is an unbelievable story.

I had been at the Strauss station about two and a half years when Crosset informed me that the Chief Patrol Inspector wanted to see me the next day. Before continuing with the story, I want to make a few remarks about Chief McBee. He didn't have much formal education, but he was well read and a fair and competent supervisor. He was probably one of the best supervisors that I worked for in my career. If an officer had common sense, worked hard, and had a good attitude he could overlook minor infractions, but he had little patience for officers who didn't make a good effort to do their jobs. He also could dictate a two or three page letter and not have to make any changes after it was transcribed, which is no small feat. When I reported to the Chief, he informed me that I was being promoted to Senior Patrol Inspector, and was to be transferred to the Fort Hancock station, which had an authorized force of 12 officers. I asked the Chief when I should report for duty at Fort Hancock, and his reply was, "Tomorrow."

Upon arriving in Fort Hancock, a town of approximately two hundred residents, I began looking for a house. The only house available was a three-room adobe structure with two screened porches. There was only one water spigot in the house, and it produced brackish water. The house had no cupboards, no closets, an outside toilet, and the screens for the windows and porches were all torn or loose. All of this "luxury" was available for only $8 per month. Additionally, the two men who had previously lived there had simply thrown their empty tin cans out the windows, so along with the other work needed to move in, I hauled two pickup loads of cans to the dump. I rented a room in Fort Hancock for a few weeks, and in my off-duty hours I would work on the house. I repaired all the screens; painted the concrete floors; planted some grass; and, for a shower, I placed a 25 gallon barrel on stilts outside the kitchen door, punched holes in the bottom of the barrel, and ran a hose from the spigot in the house to the barrel.

The Border Patrol Office in Fort Hancock was a very small, dirt floor room located behind the Hare General Merchandise Store. Mrs. Hare furnished us the room free of charge. Shortly after my arrival there, an apartment became vacant and we rented it for an office for $30 per month. We painted the floors, found a desk and a few other pieces of furniture, and we used my portable typewriter to process aliens that were being returned to Mexico locally. We took turns mopping the floors, as we were quite proud of our new office. Although the station had an authorized force of 12 officers, in the almost seven years I was there I don't recall ever having a full compliment of officers. I had no prior supervisory experience, so I was literally "flying by the seat of my pants". My approach was to be fair to my officers, keep them busy, and to be fair and honest with the growers that we encountered daily while checking their laborers in search of illegal aliens. This approach seemed to work. As I recall, I had only one serious personnel problem during my tenure at Fort Hancock.

Around 1947, I sensed an undercurrent among the officers, and it was a matter that I could not seem to get a handle on. One day while working with Patrol Inspector Dennis Crotty, I asked him if my assumption was correct, and if he knew what the problem was. He said he did, and told me that one of the officer's thought that he should be in charge of the station and was bad-mouthing and trying to undermine me. The officer in question was at the office so I immediately went to see him and told him what I had heard. He denied the allegations, and I told him that Crotty was outside in the car, and I would bring him in to confirm what I had told him. He then started crying and he cried and he kept crying. I was sorry that he took it so hard, but the encounter ended the problem.

The Fort Hancock Station included all of Hudspeth County, Texas, and some 120 miles of the border with

Mexico. Just north of the croplands were sand hills where we would cut sign daily looking for tracks of aliens who had entered the United States during the night hours. One of my officers often asked me to work the sand hills, and I was glad to oblige, as he had a stern disposition and he and the farmers definitely didn't get along. The area where he worked had a train depot with a female telegrapher and a water tower for the trains. One day this officer came to me and stated that he had had an affair with the female telegrapher and that she was pregnant. I was at a loss as to what action I should take, so I let it simmer for a while. During this time his wife returned to her home in Michigan and got a divorce from the officer. He then married the telegrapher. I did not make an issue of the officer's misconduct, and the last time I saw him he was still married to her.

About 1945, I received a call from headquarters telling me that a new officer and his wife, from Illinois, would be arriving in Fort Hancock on the 11:00 p.m. passenger train. At the time of the train's arrival, my wife and I were attending a community dance at the High School auditorium. I left the dance to meet the train, and since there was no hotel or motel in Fort Hancock, I took the couple to our 3-bedroom house that we had recently rented. They stayed for a couple of weeks, and since there were no rental houses available, the officer who had recently married the telegrapher, decided to move in with her, and the Illinois couple was able to rent his apartment. Several of us pitched in and cleaned the apartment, calcimined the walls, and when we had finished they were able to move in. About two weeks later, the Illinois officer came to me and said that his wife was not happy with her living conditions and he would have to resign. I asked if I could talk with her, and he readily consented. I told her that her husband would not have to spend his career in Fort Hancock, and that there were other stations that had much better living conditions. She replied, *"Mr. Coppock, in Illinois the chickens have better places to live than the people do in Fort Hancock."* From her comment, I realized that further talk was useless, and her husband resigned that same day.

There was another officer that I will call "Bud". He lived on the outskirts of Fort Hancock, and although he wasn't the brightest kid on the block, he was loyal and he had a good attitude. It was the custom for officers to take the government cars to their homes if they were not needed on the next shift. One day, after working his shift, Bud drove the car to his home and, as usual, took the keys in the house and hung them on a rack. That evening he and his wife went to visit friends, leaving their six children at home. The oldest of them was a boy, and he took the keys from the rack, loaded his five sisters in the government car, and drove them around the house, going faster each round. On about the fifth round, he lost control and drove the car directly into a tree, damaging the car extensively. The next day Bud came to my house and told me what had happened. I told him to take the car to headquarters and to inform the Chief of what had occurred. Knowing the Chief's concern about the proper care of government vehicles, Bud asked me to accompany him. I declined and told him that he would have to face the Chief alone. As I recall, he had to pay for the repair of the vehicle.

Soon thereafter, during World War II he was working the evening shift and unbeknown to me, he apprehended an alien entering the U.S. with a 50-pound sack of sugar. Sugar was scarce during the war, and it was being rationed. The next day Bud was drinking a cup of coffee at a café in Acala, Texas. While drinking his coffee, he stated that he had solved his sugar problem. Someone asked him how, and Bud replied that he had apprehended an alien who was smuggling a 50-pound bag of sugar across the border. Of course, this information spread up and down the valley like a wildfire. Later in the day when I heard about it, I went to Bud's house and asked him about the story I had heard. When he admitted to seizing the sugar, I instructed him to take the sugar to headquarters and declare it.

There was another officer in Fort Hancock who was a very bright and competent officer. He had six children, also, and he told me that every time he hung his pants on the bedpost his wife got pregnant. One evening while we were working together, preparing to lay-in at a well-known alien crossing, he removed the 12-gauge, sawed-off shotgun from the rack, and while in the car, shucked a shell into the chamber. As he did this, the gun went off, making a direct hit on the car radio. He, of course, had to pay for a new radio.

The work in Fort Hancock was enjoyable but challenging. Checking the growers' laborers would occasionally result in an unpleasant confrontation, as the removal of their illegal alien workers was an economic issue with them. One time while driving to El Paso with aliens, my partner, Douglas Shute, asked me if I had a Border Patrol cough drop. Naturally I asked what a Border Patrol cough drop was, and he replied that it was a tum and I had a roll. My strategy when checking farms for illegal aliens was to place officers around the farm we were checking; then I would locate the farmer and inform him that we were going to check his laborers. That way I was on the offense and the farmer was on the defense. The plan seemed to work, as I had few serious encounters with the growers.

During my tenure of almost seven years at Fort Hancock, my wife helped to establish a women's club and a library; she taught school; played the piano for the community church and the Lions Club; and she was a member of a choral group that entertained at events in the area. It is interesting to note that two of the women in that small community had graduated from the Juliard School of Music in New York. One was Patrol Inspector Gene Chaput's wife Jane. In such a small community, we had to make our own entertainment. I coached and played on the town's basketball team, and I helped establish the Fort Hancock Lions Club. I was the charter president, and I was reelected to a second term. The Lions Club organized a Lions softball team, on which I also played and coached. I also served as Scout Master for the area Boy Scouts. Shirley and I were very involved in community affairs.

After 6½ years at Fort Hancock, I learned that a new Border Patrol station was being opened in Belen, New Mexico, a town about thirty miles south of Albuquerque. I told Chief McBee that I would like to be considered for a transfer as Senior Patrol Inspector at the new station, as the schools in Fort Hancock were not very good and I had been in Fort Hancock well over 6 years. When I asked the Chief, he turned his back on me and said, *"sh.. Coppock, you don't have a chance."* Of course, this was quite a blow to my ego, as I knew that I had been doing a credible job. As I was starting a vacation, I stopped by headquarters and told the Chief that I planned to resign when I returned from my trip. He replied, *"Why didn't you tell me that you wanted to leave Fort Hancock? You can move to El Paso any time."* I learned later that the Chief had been told who would get the job in Belen. The officer who got the job had used politics, and Chief McBee was told who would fill the position. Upon returning to work I did not submit my resignation, but accepted the offer to transfer to El Paso. When we left Fort Hancock, the community had a farewell party for us and gave us a set of glasses that matched Shirley's dishes. They told us that we were the first Border Patrol family that they had given a farewell party, and that it would possibly be the last.

Our first house in Fort Hancock – a kitchen, bedroom and sitting room. There was only one spigot of water in the house, no cupboards, no closets and an outside privy. And we got all of this luxury for $8.00 per month.

Chapter Four
My Rise in the Border Patrol

In late 1949, we moved to El Paso. On my first day of duty I worked the 8:00 a.m. to 4:00 p.m. shift. The next day I was assigned to the 10:00 p.m. to 6:00 a.m. shift, and I worked night shifts for the next 3 or 4 months while in El Paso. The Chief certainly showed me who was the boss. One day the Chief summoned me to his office and asked me if I would like to transfer to the Fabens, Texas Station as the Senior Patrol Inspector, adding that the station's area of operation was rife with illegal aliens and he wanted me to clean up the area. This came as a complete surprise, and I was most happy to accept the offer.

Upon reporting for duty at Fabens, I first observed the pattern of operations. The officers were reluctant to check the growers' laborers, as there had previously been a serious conflict with one of the growers. The night shift officers usually stopped to eat at a small café in the little town of San Elazario, and during their meal they would drink two or three beers. I put a stop to this, and we began regularly checking the growers' laborers. As I stated above, before I was transferred to Fabens there had been a serious incident with a grower. This grower weighed some 400 pounds, and when you met him on the road you could tell it was he as his car leaned sharply to the left. During the altercation with this grower, he had bitten off part of an officer's ear lobe. One day while working with Patrol Inspector B. Warren O'Neill, I asked him if this grower's laborers had been checked since the incident. When he told me that they had not, I turned the car around and went directly to the grower's farm. I knocked on his door, and I told him that we were going to check his workers. He wasn't happy about it, but we were able to apprehend two illegal aliens, and one escaped. Sometime later, the grower and I became well acquainted.

With the help of my officers, we were able to drastically reduce the number of illegal aliens in the Fabens area of operation. However, I had one veteran officer to whom I had assigned an area of operation to check for illegal aliens. Daily he and his partner failed to apprehend any aliens, and when I asked him about it, he told me that his area did not have any illegals. After a few days, I assigned him to fueling the vehicles and to the processing of aliens. The officers that were assigned to that officer's area of operation apprehended illegal aliens on practically every farm that they checked.

We enjoyed our stay in Fabens as it was considerably larger than Fort Hancock; the schools were better; and the work was challenging but enjoyable. I had been in Fabens about two years and while I was moving from one house to another, the telephone rang and I sat on the floor to answer it. It was Chief McBee and he asked me if I would like to be considered for a promotion to Assistant Chief Patrol Inspector in El Paso. I immediately recalled an incident at sector headquarters when the Chief, standing on the stairs, shook his finger at the Assistant Chief and said, " *You are the dumbest one son-of-a-bitch that I ever saw in my life.* " In view of this, I told the Chief that I didn't want to be considered for the job, and that I was happy with my work in Fabens. McBee then said that I had better reconsider my decision, as it is not often that you get such an opportunity. Before our conversation ended, I agreed that I would like to be considered for the job. I was informed later that my selection had already been decided.

I commuted from Fabens to El Paso for a short time, and in 1953 we bought a house in the El Paso area. We lived in the house for a little over a year. This short stay will be discussed later. Earlier that year, the District Director, who was a very heavy drinker and who had apparently got his job through politics, gave a speech at the El Paso Growers Association, hinting that the growers didn't have to use legal aliens that were admitted under the "Bracero Program" to pick their cotton, if they could get it picked cheaper by using illegal aliens. At the time the Bracero Program, which was enacted into law during World War II when laborers were scarce, was still in effect. It provided that growers could contract Mexicans to work on their farms, as long as they paid an agreed upon wage and provided adequate housing. I knew of the District Director's speech, as I had heard rumors, and the President of the El Paso Growers Association, a friend of mine named Bud Moore who had lived in the Fort Hancock area when I was stationed there, told me about the speech. He also told me that some of the growers, knowing of the District Director's addiction to alcohol, would occasionally leave a case of whiskey on his doorstep. In view of the District Director's speech, the growers stopped using legally admitted Mexican aliens and began using illegals to pick their cotton. As Assistant Chief, I was assigned to work with the outstations to help them round up and apprehend the increasing number of illegal aliens being hired by the growers. So many illegals were being apprehended that you could hardly walk through headquarters of an evening. The jails were full, and we were limited as to the number of aliens that we could prosecute. I met with Chief McBee and told him that the growers were going to get their cotton picked by illegal aliens unless we did something different. I suggested that we take adult males that were from the interior of Mexico and repeat offenders to Columbus, New Mexico, and return them to Mexico there so that they would not be able to return to their jobs the next day. I also suggested that juveniles and women repeat offenders be returned to Mexico at a port of entry some 10 to 15 miles from their homes. Chief McBee thought that was a good idea, but stated that we should take the adult males to Presidio, Texas for expulsion, as there was a road to the interior of Mexico at that location. The next day Mr. McBee and I met with the Deputy District Director, Merle Toole, to discuss the plan, as the District Director was on a detail to the Central Office in Washington, D. C. Mr. Toole was very much in favor of the idea, but we had a problem. We all knew that if the District Director knew of the plan he would not approve. Mr. Toole said that maybe he could get the District Director's detail extended and if so, we could get the plan in operation before his return to El Paso. It sounds like we were attempting something subversive, but for us it was something that needed to be done. Mr. Toole called the Commissioner of the Immigration and Naturalization Service in Washington D.C., explained our plan, and the Commissioner agreed to extend the District Director's detail. Because of my previous experience, I was given the job of making the arrangements for buses to be used to transport the aliens to Presidio, Texas. Chief McBee had contacted the Chief in Marfa, told him of our plan, and asked him to contact the officials in Ojinaga, Chihuahua, Mexico, which was just across the border from Presidio, and asked them what would be the best time for the buses to arrive at the border. Since a freight train would depart from Ojinaga at 8:00 a.m., he said the buses should arrive there around 7:00 a.m., and we could drive to the depot and put the aliens on the train before it departed for Chihuahua City, which was located about 350 miles from the Texas border. In the meantime, I contacted officials at the Fort Bliss Army Base and arranged to borrow buses until we were able to charter buses for the operation. When the District Director returned to El Paso he was not happy, but he did not try to stop the operation. Within about 10 days the growers were asking, even begging for permission to hire Mexican aliens admitted under the terms of the Bracero Program. Sending the illegals to the interior of Mexico in this manner vividly illustrates what can be accomplished by taking the profit out of the aliens' illegal entry. Putting it another way, almost 100% of the Mexican aliens who enter the United

States illegally do so to improve their economic status. If you make it uneconomical for them to enter the United States illegally, they will stay home! After most of the illegals were removed from the El Paso area of operation, I was detailed to Van Horn, Texas, along with 18 other officers, to check the laborers working on farms in that area. When we were finished there, we moved to Del City, Texas, for the same purpose. After we checked the farms, we went to the cotton gin and checked the laborers working there. Almost all of the workers in the gin were illegal aliens. After they were apprehended, I met with the gin manager in his office. He told me that the District Director had told him if he had any problems with the Border Patrol to call him, and the gin manager pointed to the District Director's telephone number that was written on the wall beside his desk. I said, *"Please, be my guest and call him."* But, the manager refused the offer.

Within a few days, the Central Office sent a representative to El Paso to investigate the above-mentioned infractions. The representative interviewed the others and I who were involved. Shortly after that, the District Director was demoted and transferred to Miami, Florida, as the Deputy District Director. Marcus Neeley, a bright, well-qualified enforcement official, replaced him as the District Director for the El Paso area. Mr. Neeley taught Naturalization Law when I attended the Border Patrol Training School thirteen years earlier. On one Saturday shortly after he reported for duty, he came to my office and asked me to drive him around and help him get acquainted with the area. He also questioned me about the previous District Director's actions that had caused his demotion. Mr. Neeley was aware of the growers' need for workers, and before permitting them to hire Mexican laborers legally admitted under the Bracero program, he required each grower to come to his office and sign an agreement stating that they would not hire any illegal aliens.

As of 2006, there were an estimated twelve million illegal aliens in the United States. Although the President took an oath that he would uphold the laws of the United States, he has done little to enforce the immigration laws. I am at a loss to understand how this has happened. The Border Patrol force has been increased from about 1,600 officers when I was Chief of the United States Border Patrol, to nearly 13,000 officers at present. The President recently criticized the Border Patrol for apprehending illegal aliens who were employed, stating that they should concentrate their efforts on apprehending criminals and terrorists. It is the Border Patrol's statutory authority to apprehend aliens that are here illegally, whether they are employed or not. He also criticized the group of citizens called the Minute Men, who were watching the border to detect illegal entries; he called them vigilantes. Most all of the Mexican aliens entering illegally are poor and uneducated. While we feel sorry about their circumstances, they are causing a severe economic strain, not only on the border states, but in other states as well, because of the increased cost of treating indigent aliens in emergency rooms and their stay in hospitals; the increase in welfare payments; the increase in school enrollments; and the increase in crimes committed by aliens. Almost 31% of criminals in our penitentiaries are illegal aliens. It is absolute madness to let this insane policy continue. This administration and the congress talk of raising the Border Patrol force to twenty thousand officers. While this would help, it is not the answer. They are also talking of building some 700 miles of fence, which would cost billions of dollars and would take years to complete. The answer to the illegal alien problem is really quite simple. Provide gathering/holding facilities at two or three locations along the Mexico border for the Mexican aliens that have been apprehended; fly adult male aliens who come from the interior of Mexico and adult repeat offenders to a port of entry many miles from the border. Juvenile and female repeat offenders would be returned to Mexico at a port of entry ten to twenty miles from their homes. This procedure is humane and effective as it takes the profit away from Mexican aliens entering the United States illegally. The effectiveness of this practice will be illustrated later in the book when speaking about Border Patrol operations.

As mentioned, we bought a house in the El Paso area and moved there in April of 1953; but we lived there only a little over a year. In early May of 1954, I was in Denver, Colorado, interviewing applicants who had applied for a job in the Border Patrol. The second night there I became very ill, and about 5:30 the next morning the hotel doctor diagnosed my illness as appendicitis. He said he would arrange for me to be transported to the hospital, as I needed to have my appendix removed immediately. I told him that if I had to have an operation, I would prefer it be done in El Paso. I informed him that there was a plane departing Denver at 8:00 a.m. and it would arrive in El Paso about 12:00 noon. The doctor reluctantly agreed to let me fly to El Paso on the condition that I hold an ice pack over my appendix during the entire flight. My wife, Shirley, met my plane and took me directly to St. Mary's Hospital where our family doctor was waiting. He helped prepare me for the operation, and accompanied me to the operating room where we waited for the surgeon who was to perform the operation. As I lay there looking at all the surgical tools neatly arranged on the table beside me, my doctor sensed my nervousness and tried to avert my attention by asking me what I thought of my new boss. I thought he was referring to Marcus Neeley the new District Director, and I told him Mr. Neeley was a very likable and competent official. He replied that he had been talking about General Joe Swing, who had recently been appointed by President Eisenhower as Commissioner of the Immigration Service. I said, *"Commissioners come and go, and they have little effect on the officers working in the field."* I couldn't have been more wrong! The doctor told me he had served under General Swing in the Army, and that somehow I would feel his presence. How right he was! I never worked another shift in El Paso. I was in the hospital two or three days, and released to recover at home.

After a couple of days at home, I drove to Border Patrol Sector Headquarters just to get out of the house and see what was going on. Upon my arrival at headquarters, I was told that there was an important meeting in the District Director's office, and that I probably should attend. At the meeting I was told that the Commissioner, Joe Swing, was inaugurating a plan, the purpose of which was to remove the large number of illegal Mexican aliens living and working in the Los Angeles and San Antonio District Areas of Operation. The El Paso District, which included the Marfa, El Paso and Tucson sectors, had relatively few illegal aliens working in their areas. They called the operation the 1954 Wet Back Drive. It would not be politically correct at this day and time to refer to illegal Mexican aliens as "wetbacks". I assume that because the El Paso Border Patrol sector had done such an effective job of ridding its area of operation of illegal aliens, many officers from the sector were chosen to run/supervise the Wet Back Drive. Two days after the meeting on May 22, 1954, a Border Patrol plane flew Chief G. J. McBee and me to El Centro, California, where many others and we met with Harlon Carter, Chief of the U. S. Border Patrol. Meetings were held continuously to strategize as to how the "drive" would be conducted. It was determined that the El Centro Border Patrol Sector Headquarters would be the gathering point for aliens that were apprehended, as it was centrally located and had a detention facility. The number of officers needed was determined, and Border Patrol officers and investigators from all over the United States were detailed to the area. It was decided that officers would be assigned to 12 man groups, with each group having a supervisor and an assistant.

I didn't know at the time, but it was the beginning of my rise in the ranks of the Border Patrol. To this day

I do not know precisely what brought about my rapid promotions, but I attribute it largely to my suggestion that illegal Mexican aliens be removed to the interior of Mexico so as to take the profit out of their coming here illegally, since most come here to improve their economic status. Before the operation was activated, Chief McBee and I were detailed to Sacramento, California to formulate a plan of operation for Northern California. The first night we were there we drove by the State Capital Building and we observed a Mexican sitting on the Capital Building steps. We stopped and, upon questioning him, we found out that he was an illegal alien. It was probably the first apprehension of the operation.

After our task was completed in Northern California, we returned to El Centro. I was assigned to arrange for the bus lifts, keep track of the number of aliens arriving in El Centro, selecting those aliens to be sent on the bus lift, and at the end of the day provide the total number of aliens bus lifted and the number of buses used. As planned the aliens were bused to the Port of Entry at Sonora, Arizona, and from there to Santa Ana, Sonora, Mexico, a town about 150 miles from the border. We were working at least 12 hours a day and in view of my recent operation, it was difficult, but I survived.

About two weeks after the operation started, I was transferred to the Chula Vista, California Border Patrol Sector as acting Chief Patrol Inspector. The Chief in Chula Vista, Joe Vanorshovon, had been detailed to Grand Forks, North Dakota as the Acting Chief of that sector. I was informed that I could choose my Assistant

Chief, and I selected Senior Patrol Inspector Edward Smith from the El Paso Sector since I had worked with him and knew him to be intelligent, loyal and a hard worker. He later became Chief of the Marfa, Texas Sector. My wife Shirley and our daughter Mary-Blue joined me in Chula Vista. We found an inexpensive apartment, and instead of eating our evening meal in the apartment, we would usually go to the beach where I could take a swim and we would cook fresh vegetables on a gas grill. It was an awesome experience, as we had lived our lives in the interior and flatlands of the United States.

While I was still Acting Chief Patrol Inspector in Chula Vista, Chief Joe Vanorshovon returned; however I was still in charge of the sector. It was a somewhat uncomfortable situation, but Vanorshovon handled it well. Occasionally we would go to a bar after work to visit and have a couple of drinks. The work in Chula Vista was quite challenging, as there was generally a morning fog until around 11:00 a.m.; consequently the Border Patrol planes could not fly until the fog lifted. However, there were two officers who rode horseback along the border starting at daylight, and at the end of their shift they would report the number and locations of illegal entries. The weather in Chula Vista was heavenly, especially when compared to the hot weather we experienced in El Centro where in the summer the temperature could be 100 degrees at midnight.

In August of 1954, I was transferred and promoted to Chief Patrol Inspector in El Centro, California. The Chief of that sector, Ed Parker, was also a pilot, and he had been transferred to supervise and fly the Patrol's transport aircraft. Control of the illegal aliens' entry into that sector area of operations was quite simple. The All American Canal, which carried water from the Colorado River to the Imperial Valley, ran parallel to the border and was very deep and quite swift. Accordingly, illegal aliens entering the United States would cross at one of the five bridges that crossed the canal. Soon after I arrived in El Centro, General Frank Partridge, head of enforcement for the Immigration Service, made an inspection of the El Centro Border Patrol Sector. I had a very crude drawing of the All American Canal that showed the location of the five bridges, and I explained to the General that the illegal entry problem in that sector could be controlled as long as I had enough officers to guard the bridges 24 hours a day. I'm fairly certain that this inspection helped me immensely in my career, as my stay in El Centro was quite brief. Officers from the El Paso District filled many of the supervisory positions in the newly established regional offices. I recall some of the California officers and others remarking that *"the only good thing that came out of Texas was Highway 80."*

Calexico, California was an out station of the El Centro Sector that was situated adjacent to the Mexican border. In addition to watching the bridges across the All American Canal, the Calexico officers were assigned to cover the bus station 24 hours a day, as buses departed Calexico frequently for the interior of the United States. A couple of times while visiting the station, I noticed officers escorting aliens with an excessive amount of luggage from the bus station to the Border Patrol station, which indicated the aliens were returning to Mexico. I verified this with the Senior Patrol Inspector, Carlos Sears, and I asked him if he had other officers covering the bus station while the aliens were being processed. When he replied in the negative, I suggested that he should instruct the officers to let those aliens that were returning to Mexico proceed to do so, as other aliens could be leaving the area by bus while these officers were busy processing these aliens, and we didn't need apprehensions all that bad. Several years later, when I was Chief of the Border Patrol, I was on an inspection trip to the El Centro Sector and I found that same situation was occurring at the Indio, California Station. I talked to the Chief, George Harrison, about letting those aliens that were encountered returning to Mexico to proceed on their own. His reply was a vehement, *"Hell, no! If aliens were in the United States illegally they should be apprehended."* George was one of my supporters when I was promoted to Assistant Chief in El Paso, and the idea of taking a suggestion from me was probably objectionable to him. I had no choice but to accept his decision, because he was right; but in my opinion, he wasn't envisioning the big picture. While I was Chief in the El Centro Sector, I was occasionally detailed to the Regional Office as Acting Chief of the Region. I recall a couple of time while I was detailed to the region; I was able to approve recommendations that I had made at the El Centro Sector.

In 1956 my brief tenure as Chief of the El Centro Sector ended, and I was promoted to Chief of the Border in the Southwest Region, which had the responsibility for the operations along the Mexican border extending from San Diego, California to Brownsville, Texas. We bought a house in Garden Grove, and I commuted 27 miles in heavy traffic to the regional office, which was located on Terminal Island. There were four other officers living in the area, and we car-pooled, which eased the commuting problem. One of the officers, Maurice Wilce, always kept the group entertained with his wit and good humor. The Regional Commissioner, Dave Carnahan, had served with General Swing in the Army. The Deputy Regional Commissioner, Merle Toole, had been the Deputy District Director in El Paso who made it possible for us to start the El Paso to Ojinaga, Mexico bus lift. Mr. Toole actually ran the Regional Office as he was well versed in the Immigration Laws and was an outstanding supervisor and leader. John Swanson, who I had worked with in El Paso, was Regional Enforcement Officer and my immediate supervisor. We got along well, as I had always respected my supervisors. Mr. Swanson had a few problems, as we all do, but his worst problem was his drinking. Without going into detail, it is fair to say that he was fortunate his drinking didn't get him into serious trouble. In spite of this, he was a good officer.

I thoroughly enjoyed my work in the Regional Office, and I would have been happy to have spent the rest of my career there. But, after a little over a year, I was summoned to Mr. Toole's office and he informed me that I was being transferred to the Central Office in Washington, D.C. and promoted to the position as Deputy Chief of the Border Patrol. I had a feeling that this might happen, and I certainly didn't want to live east of the Mississippi River. I told Mr. Toole that I would like to talk to my wife about the transfer. Mr. Toole replied that this was not an option and that I should resign myself to the fact that I was being transferred to Washington, D.C.

I was detailed to the Central Office in Washington, D.C. for a couple of weeks, and during the time I was there I bought a house in Cheverly, Maryland, a suburb of Washington. I had paid $12,500 for my house in Garden Grove, California, and when I heard of my pending transfer, my next-door neighbor, a good friend, told me that he would buy my house for the amount I paid for it, thus eliminating the need for a real estate broker. I told him that I had spent $1,200 remodeling the kitchen, and he said for me to add that amount to the cost. Therefore, I sold our house in California for $13,700, which wasn't a very smart deal, I imagine, since that house would sell on today's market for a minimum of $1,000,000. However, I needed the money in order to buy the house in Maryland.

Driving my 1955 Ford two-door car, we left California for Washington, D.C. in late June of 1957. The trip was mostly uneventful, but I do recall a couple of interesting incidents. My wife Shirley, besides packing for the trip, had taught school right up until the time we left California. She was exhausted and slept most of the way in the back seat of the car. When we crossed the Mississippi River at St. Louis, my daughter reached back and told her to wake up because we were crossing the Mississippi. Shirley replied that she would see it some other time, and immediately went back to sleep. During our trip we also spent a few days visiting family in Oklahoma, and after leaving there we stayed three nights on the road – in Springfield, Missouri; in Springfield, Illinois; and in Springfield, Ohio. It was slow going as the Interstate Highways had not been built, and we drove through the center of each small town and large city.

Upon reporting for duty as Deputy Chief of the Border Patrol, my immediate supervisors were James F. Greene, Chief of the Border Patrol who was a very intelligent official, but who had very little experience in the Border Patrol, and General Frank Partridge, who was the Head of Enforcement for the service. Partridge had served in the Army with Commissioner Joe Swing, and was a personable and capable supervisor. One of my first assignments was to write a history of the Border Patrol from the time of its beginning on May 28, 1924 until 1957. The research took weeks, and it proved to be a valuable document as it was used at the Border Patrol Academy and was updated annually until my retirement on June 30, 1973. Also, during the first year I traveled extensively visiting Border Patrol Sectors and Stations, especially along the Canadian border and in the Florida and Gulf Coast areas. I recall visiting the New Orleans Sector with General Partridge. The Sector Chief, while driving us to sector stations, chain-smoked and got lost. Although the General didn't say anything, I could tell that he was disgusted. He was a clean living non-smoker, and he was unhappy. It wasn't long before the Chief of the New Orleans Sector was transferred to the Southwest region to a non-supervisory position. Charles Chamblee who was personable and an outstanding supervisory officer replaced him. He was a great help to the Border Patrol and me in later years when we were called upon to help enforce the civil rights statutes during the 1960s.

To my knowledge, the first effort to enroll a Negro in an all white school in the South occurred during the Eisenhower administration, when U.S. Marshalls escorted a young Negro girl into a school in Little Rock, Arkansas. John Sigenthaler, editor of the Nashville Tennessee Newspaper, was serving in the Justice Department at that time. He was detailed to represent the Department and to monitor the event. A large crowd was gathered at the school to protest the little girl's enrollment. Mr. Sigenthaler met with the leader of the crowd in an attempt to ease the tensions. Instead of talking, the leader hit Mr. Sigenthaler in the jaw and knocked him down. A few years later when I was in Nashville on business, I met with Mr. Sigenthaler in his office, and he was able to laugh about what happened. That incident was an indication of how strong southerners felt about desegregation at that time.

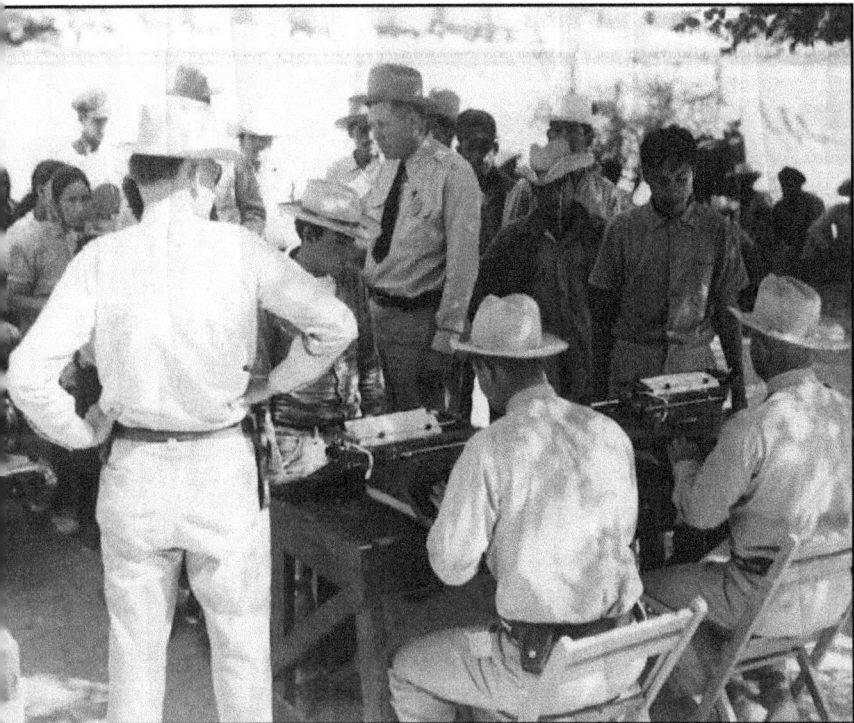

Processing Mexican Aliens at Fabens, Texas, in 1953 before they were bus-lifted to Presidio, Texas, and returned to Mexico.

Chapter Five
Ole Miss/James Meredith

In 1960 I was promoted to the position as Chief of the U. S. Border Patrol. At that time the "Bracero" program was in operation. The program permitted growers to hire legally admitted Mexican laborers. The laborers were paid a guaranteed wage as provided in the agreement with the Mexican government. Because of the program, the illegal entry of Mexican aliens was not considered a major problem as the apprehensions of illegals were in the area of 50,000 per year.

In early May 1961, the Department of Justice asked the Border Patrol to prepare plans to assist the Department in quelling the racial strife that was expected to occur in Montgomery, Alabama. On May 22, 1962, I was directed to send 341 Patrol Inspectors, 99 vehicles, an airplane, 53 handie-talkies, and a base radio station to Montgomery. I was not personally involved, so I don't have details regarding the operation. However, the officers must have done their work well, as peace was restored and the detail was terminated on May 30. This was the first of many times that the Border Patrol was called upon to help the Department enforce the civil rights statutes.

Subsequent to the Montgomery disturbance, I was

informed that the Border Patrol would probably be asked to provide assistance at several locations in the South where civil strife was expected. Accordingly, we initiated a training program that indoctrinated our officers in the procedures and techniques in riot control situations. Additionally, detailed plans were to furnish up to 300 officers, 42 radio equipped vehicles, and 40 handie-talkies radios if needed. The Chief Patrol Inspector of the Miami, Florida Sector, Elmo Rainbolt, and the Chief Patrol Inspector of the New Orleans Sector, Charles Chamblee, were selected as field supervisors who would assist me in carrying out any requests made by the Attorney General. Plans were also made for all officers to be sworn in as Deputy U. S. Marshalls. Riot equipment (tear gas, smoke grenades, gas masks, helmets, etc.) stored at the New Orleans Border Patrol Sector would be brought to the area of operation.

On Friday, September 7, 1962, a meeting was held in the office of Assistant Deputy Attorney General William A. Geoghegan concerning the possibility of civil strife when James Meredith, a black student who had been attending a community college in Jackson, Mississippi, would attempt to enroll at the University of Mississippi (Ole Miss) at the start of school on September 21, and the possible need for help from the Border Patrol. Present at the meeting were officials from the Department of Justice, the United States Marshalls Office, and Mr. James Greene and myself from the Immigration Service. Tentative plans were made for U. S. Marshalls, prison guards, and some 300 Border Patrol officers to meet at the Millington Naval Air Base near Memphis,

Tennessee to facilitate the enrollment of James Meredith, if assistance were needed. A court order to permit Meredith's enrollment was denied, then appealed to an appellate court, which upheld Meredith's right to enroll at the university. Accordingly, my staff prepared detailed plans to comply with the department's request.

It was soon learned that Mississippi officials did not intend to comply with the court order. The Kennedy administration was clear in its intention to end segregation and that James Meredith would be enrolled at the University of Mississippi. In late September, I was informed that the Border Patrol would be needed. In accordance with the order, a total of 314 Border Patrol officers, including radio technicians, were detailed to the Millington Naval Air Base. Also provided were 45 radio-equipped vehicles, five transport planes and two observation planes. In addition, some 100 U. S. Marshalls and prison guards were detailed to the operation. On September 27, I flew to Memphis where Chief Patrol Inspector Charles Chamblee met me. He was well liked, a leader and a very capable officer who played a major roll in the "Ole Miss" crisis and other disturbances. I referred to him as my field general.

At a meeting that evening, I was selected to supervise the approximately 400 officers, although Border Patrol Officers were sworn in as U. S. Marshals for the civil rights events taking place. During the next two days, with the help of Charles Chamblee, we took a "page" from the "wetback drive" of 1954. We organized all of the officers into groups of 12 men and designated a supervisor and assistant for each group. A handie-talkie radio was issued to each supervisor, and they were instructed that when they arrived on the campus of "Ole Miss" they were to surround the Lyceum building. It was the location on campus where James Meredith was to be enrolled.

Knowing that we would not be welcome in Oxford, Mississippi and that there weren't enough motel spaces to accommodate our entire complement of men, the army set up what was referred to as "Tent City". All of us were provided eating and sleeping facilities at that location.

While still at the Millington Naval Base, a young patrol officer asked to speak with me. He stated that he was from Alabama, that his heart was not in our mission, and that he would like to be relieved from the detail and return to his duty station. After asking him to have a seat, I explained to him that when he entered the Border Patrol he had taken an oath to uphold and enforce the laws of the United States, and that we were there to enforce a lawful court order. He reluctantly agreed to stay and perform the job required of him on this mission. Ironically, after the crisis at "Ole Miss" was over, I needed a few officers to remain a couple of days longer to handle some unfinished business and this young officer volunteered to stay. I believe that when he saw the actions of the students and other members of the mob and heard the vindictive slurs that were directed at us, he realized the worthiness of our efforts.

There was indecision as to when would be the best time to move the operation to Oxford. About 1:00 p.m. on Sunday, September 30, 1962, it was decided that we should have a dry run, so all of the officers would know what to do when the order was given to move to Oxford. Officers that were to go by air were loaded on planes, and those that were to drive went to their vehicles. The "Ole Miss" football team played a game out of town that weekend, and many students were not on campus. During the dry run, Attorney General Robert Kennedy and President John Kennedy decided that it was the best time to activate the operation. Since it was supposed to be a dry run not all of the twelve-officer units stayed together as had been requested, but they were able to get together upon arriving at Oxford.

We departed the Millington Naval Air Base about 1:45 p.m., arriving at Oxford at 2:20 p.m. A supply of tear gas was also moved to the Oxford airport. The officers arriving by air were transported by bus to the "Ole Miss" campus, and when they arrived about 4:00 p.m., they surrounded the Lyceum building. Deputy Attorney General Nicholas Katzenbach was ensconced inside the building. Upon his arrival there, he had placed a call to the President, leaving the line open all during the night so the President and Attorney General could be kept informed of the situation.

Assistant Attorney General Louis Oberdorfer and I went to the basement of the Courthouse, along with a radio technician who set up the base radio station. Patrol Inspectors Carl Endress and Charles Williams also accompanied us. This was to be our command center for the operation. The first radio communication occurred at 5:20 p.m. when I was informed that a fifteen car convoy of Border Patrol cars, lead by Patrol Inspector James Story, had arrived at the airport. I requested that they immediately move to the campus. One of the cars, from Gulfport, Mississippi, had a highway patrol radio, which became a valuable tool as it enabled us to follow their actions and learn whether they were going to help or hinder us. The latter eventually became true.

At 5:35 p.m. I was informed that a crowd of two to three hundred people had gathered near the Lyceum building. At 6:00 p.m. Border Patrol Pilot Don Harrison landed his plane at the Oxford airport with James Meredith, Assistant Attorney General John Doar, and U. S. Marshal Miller on board. Meredith was taken immediately by car to Baxter Hall on the campus of "Ole Miss". At 6:15 p.m. a convoy of Border Patrol cars and trucks arrived on campus with a highway patrol car leading the way. Realizing the significance of the operation, I had Assistant Chief Patrol Inspector Carl Endress (from the Spokane, Washington Border Patrol Sector) keep a log of each radio and telephone message sent and received, and the time each message occurred. I kept a copy of this log, and it has been a valuable tool in providing a record of the events as they happened.

At 7:30 p.m. I was informed that the crowd at the campus was growing larger and uglier. In addition to the profane and insulting language directed at the officers, they were throwing bricks and other objects at them. There was a supply of bricks across the street from the campus where a building was under construction, and the crowd was using those bricks. At this time, I learned that a broken coke bottle had hit a Deputy Marshal. He was transported to a local hospital where he was treated. At 7:45 p.m., in an attempt to subdue the crowd that was becoming more unruly and dangerous, the first tear gas was discharged. By 8:15 p.m. the officers had used all of their tear gas, and more had to be brought from the airport. At 10:15 p.m. I was informed that a state Highway Patrol Officer had been hit with a tear gas canister. He required hospitalization, and I had him flown by Border Patrol Plane to Jackson, Mississippi for treatment, since the local hospital could not give him the attention he needed.

It was at this time that I was informed by Chief Patrol Inspectors Elmo Rainbolt and Charles Chamblee, my field supervisors, that the crowd was now getting even more dangerous as they were throwing bricks, pipes, rocks and anything they could find at the officers. Additionally, I was told that a rioter or rioters had fired shots at our officers. An officer asked me by radio if they could return fire. It was a difficult decision, but I informed the officer that under no circumstances could they return fire. He then asked what they were supposed to do, and I told him that, if the shooting continued, they should lie down with their hard hats facing the shooters. Some members of the crowd commandeered a fire truck and tried to run over the officers. Other members started a bulldozer and ran it towards the officers. Luckily, no one was hit. One member of the crowd was shot on campus. He was carried to the Lyceum building and later taken to a local hospital where he died. Many of the officers were injured, and Patrol Inspectors George Branch and Steve Donnelly were shot.

They were awarded the Border Patrol equivalent of the Purple Heart at our retiree conference in El Paso, Texas in 2005. At about 11:00 p.m. a doctor arrived at the Lyceum building where he treated many of the injured officers.

The officers were running short of tear gas, and Pilot Don Harrison, who had picked up forty additional cases at Millington Naval Air Station, arrived back at the Oxford airport a little after 11:00 p.m. Chief Patrol Inspector Charles Chamblee and a helper picked up the tear gas and, while returning to the campus, were stopped by some local police and Highway Patrol officers who claimed they were speeding and tried to seize the tear gas. Chamblee and his helper fought them off using their nightsticks, and after quite a struggle they were able to get to the campus. The gas was sorely needed, since protestors from all over the South were converging near the campus. General Edwin Walker, a Texan who had headed the Army unit that enabled a black girl to enroll in Central High School in Little Rock, Arkansas in 1957 during the Eisenhower administration, had arrived in Oxford. During the Little Rock crisis he had stated: "*As an Officer of the Unites States Army, I have been chosen to command these forces and to execute the President's orders. We are all subject to the law, whether we approve of it or not, and as law abiding citizens we have an obligation to obey them. There can be no exceptions; if it were otherwise, we would not be a nation, but an unruly mob.*" In 1961 General Walker resigned from the Army after being reprimanded for indoctrinating his troops with right wing propaganda. On

September 26, 1962, after hearing of James Meredith's intention to enroll at Mississippi University, he made an appearance on a call-in-radio talk show at a Shreeveport, Louisiana station. During the program, he made a plea to keep "Ole Miss" segregated, stating that now is the time to be heard; rally to the cause of freedom; bring your tents and skillets to Oxford. He concluded his statements by saying that, *"I am on the other side of the issue than at a place called Little Rock, and I was on the wrong side."* Walker and his group were ensconced a short distance from the campus.

At 11:50 p.m. I received word that a French reporter had been shot and killed. Arrangements had been made for the 101st Airborne Division from Fort Benning, Georgia, headed by General Charles Billingslea, to be on standby status to help control the situation if their services were needed. They were supposed to have a forty-five minute response time. Shortly after the two officers were shot and the first man was killed, the military was asked to immediately move to the campus. By 11:30 p.m. the military had not arrived. At this time I received a call from Attorney General Robert Kennedy, who was in the Oval Office with the President, who asked me if I was in touch with General Billingslea. While he was still on the line I called Chief Patrol Inspector Elmo Rainbolt and asked him if he knew the whereabouts of General Billingslea. He replied that he was in the car with him. I told him to stand by, that I had a message for the General from the President. I told Mr. Kennedy that I was in touch with the General, and he said to take down this message and relay it to the General word-for-word. The message read: *"People are being shot and killed on the campus of Mississippi University. This is the worst thing I have heard in all of my 45 years. You were supposed to have a 45-minute response time if your help was needed. It has now been hours since you were notified. I want you to get off you ass and move now!"* After receiving the message, I radioed Rainbolt and asked him if the General could call me by phone, as I hated to relay the message by radio. A few minutes later I received a phone call from the General and read the President's message to him. I saw the General about two years later and, during our conversation, I mentioned that he had had a pretty rough night in Oxford. He replied, *"I did, but I have another star on my shoulder, so it wasn't too bad."* About an hour after I relayed the President's message to the General, the 101st Airborne Division marched to the campus in lockstep formation with rifles at the ready. Even though the military was late, they did it right, and upon their arrival, the crowd dispersed and the long night at "Ole Miss" was finally over.

Shortly after daylight, I went to the campus and it looked like a war zone. Bullet marks were visible on the massive doors of the Lyceum building, and trash and tear gas canisters littered the area. I found that seventy-seven officers had been injured, and thirteen Border Patrol vehicles had their windows knocked out. Later that day James McShane asked for four volunteers to stay in Oxford a few more days to guard Baxter Hall, the dormitory where Mr. Meredith was living. To my surprise one of the volunteers was the Patrol Inspector who had asked me to be relieved from the detail. Another volunteer was Patrol Inspector James Burns. He wrote me that during the remainder of the night and during their stay, students brought them coffee, blankets and news about what was happening. He further stated that Trent Lott was one of the students; he later became a Senator from Mississippi and was at one time chosen as Senate Majority Leader. He also wrote that one of the most beautiful sounds he had ever heard was the lock-step cadence of the 101st Airborne Division coming down that brick street to the campus. Additionally, he wrote that he had no desire to live through another such experience, but that it was something he took great pride in. He said that he was proud of the Border Patrol, and that he was proud of his Chief Patrol Inspector, Charles Chamblee.

When my supervisor, James Greene, called that morning, I told him that Chief Chamblee had done outstanding work during the night, and I suggested that he be recognized for his work. Later that day he was flown to Washington, D.C. where he was commended and thanked by the Commissioner of the Immigration Service, Raymond Farrell, his deputy James Greene, and by Attorney General Robert Kennedy. (See photo) I received another letter from Patrol Inspector Burns stating that he was proud of the way all of the Border Patrol Officers had conducted themselves during the "Ole Miss" crisis. He also told me that while on another detail to help quell civil strife in Montgomery, Alabama, a cross was burned near his home and a preacher had stated from the pulpit that "they ought to lynch that black buzzard", referring to Martin Luther King. Such a statement simply illustrates - again - the strong feelings people in the South had about desegregation at that time. Burns also stated that when his convoy arrived at the campus and they drove around the circle in front of the Lyceum building, he remembered thinking that he had never seen such beautiful women using such foul language, and the night got uglier.

The day after that fateful night, arrangements were made with a body shop in Memphis, Tennessee to replace the windows and windshields that had been broken out of the Border Patrol vehicles by the protestors. Before the convoy departed for Memphis, I told the Senior Patrol Inspector in charge of the operation to not bring back any liquor, as Oxford was in a dry county, and local officers could possibly be on the lookout for any legal violations we might commit. On their way to Memphis the convoy was observed by officers of Holly Springs, Mississippi, a town about thirty miles north of Oxford. That evening Sheriff's deputies had set up a roadblock stopping all cars going south. The first two Border Patrol cars passed through without incident, but the third car had a bottle of liquor lying on the back seat. The officers were held, and their identification cards were seized. When I received word about what had happened, I sent Chief Patrol Inspector Charles Chamblee and Assistant Chief Patrol Inspector Herbert Walsh to Holly Springs to deal with the problem. Thank goodness they were successful in getting the officers released and having their identification cards returned. By October 3rd, things had more or less returned to normal, and

I started releasing officers to return to their official stations. However, I had a premonition that the Holly Springs incident might rear it's ugly head again, so I had all of the officers that were on the Memphis detail assigned to leave on the first flight, which was scheduled to depart at 2:00 p.m. At approximately 2:30 p.m., two Sheriff's deputies from Holly Springs contacted me at Tent City. The deputies informed me that they had warrants of arrest for several officers. They showed me a list of the names and asked me to produce them. I told them they were free to try and locate them, but that I wasn't going to do it for them. I realize this might be hard to believe, but it is absolutely true. At the time I was talking to the deputies, I heard the Border Patrol plane taking off. The last I saw of the deputies they were milling around among the remaining officers trying to find their "suspects". An embarrassing, possibly national, incident had been avoided.

Later, a student at "Ole Miss" sued the government alleging that the Border Patrol Officers had injured him during the melee. After many depositions were taken from the officers, the case was finally dismissed.

On October 5th, I boarded a plane in Memphis for my return trip to Washington, D.C. On the same flight was John Doar, Assistant Attorney General in charge of the Civil Rights Division of the Department. During the trip, he asked me how many Negroes we had in the Border Patrol. When I replied that we had none, he suggested that we should hire some and start integrating the organization. Over the next couple of years I, along with members of my staff, visited nearly all of the "colored" universities in the United States. The students at these universities seemed very interested, but only a few followed through and were hired.

In September 1978, thirty-four recently retired Border Patrol Officers met in Denver, Colorado for the purpose of establishing a fraternal organization comprised of former colleagues. After several meetings and a considerable amount of discussion, the FRATERNAL ORDER OF BORDER OFFICERS (FORBPO) was born. Officers for the organization were elected, and it was decided that we would meet annually at different locations across the country. At the conclusion of our 2006 conference in Phoenix, Arizona, I asked all of the officers who had been involved in the "Ole Miss" episode to meet for a photograph. (See Photo) I later sent each one a copy of the photo, and I asked them to write about their experiences and thoughts about the Oxford operation. The most interesting letter about the events was the one already mentioned from Patrol Inspector James Burns.

Thinking back on the Border Patrol's work and involvement in helping enforce the civil rights laws that permitted James Meredith to attend the University of Mississippi gives me many nostalgic moments. I am, and was, most pleased with the restraint and the professional manner in which the Border Patrol Inspectors conducted themselves throughout the operation. This was reflected in a statement released on October 1, 1962 by Attorney General Robert F. Kennedy. It read:

THE BORDER PATROL/MARSHALS AND THE
INTEGRATION
OF THE UNIVERSITY OF MISSISSIPPI

I think last night was the worst night I ever spent. We had these Border Patrol Officers and U. S. Marshals who, perhaps, originally signed up…not realizing that they would be involved in enrolling James Meredith as the first black student at the University of Mississippi.

They were out there with instructions not to fire. They were fired on, they were hit, things were thrown at them. It was an extremely dangerous situation.

All they had, finally, was the tear gas. We received information that the tear gas was running out, that they had only four or five minutes. The mob brought up a bulldozer and attacked the University Administration Building the officers were protecting.

And I think it was that close. If the tear gas hadn't arrived in that last five minutes, and if these men hadn't remained true to their orders and instructions, if they had lost their heads and started firing at the crowd, you would have had immense bloodshed and I think it would have been a very tragic situation.

So, to hear these reports that were coming to the President and myself all of last night…when the situation with the State Police having deserted the operation, and these men standing up there with courage and ability and great bravery…that was a very moving period in my life.

….. ROBERT F. KENNEDY

Forty years later, in 2002, there was a ceremony at the University of Mississippi celebrating the end of segregation at that institution, and the following statement was released to the press:

The University of Mississippi looks much different in 2002

than it did in 1962. Nearly thirteen percent of the student population today at "Ole Miss" is black. A special legacy remains intact as well, with James Meredith's son, Joseph, graduating in 2003 as the top doctoral student in the business school.

Since the work of the Border Patrol and the U.S. Marshals was never celebrated – and rarely mentioned – state and university officials recently made up for lost time by honoring them, as well as other law enforcement and military personnel who were involved in the safeguarding of the elder Meredith's right to attend classes at "Ole Miss". On October 1, 2002, more than two hundred people, including Director Reyna and Mississippi Governor Ronnie Musgrave, commemorated the bravery of those who stood in the way of violence and civil disobedience.

James Meredith was present as well. Meredith, 69, battling cancer, was reflective as he addressed the crowd. He was grateful for those who protected him and the federal government's rule of law. *"I thought the fact that the enforcement officers and the military followed the command of the authority of the United States was what made today possible."* He said, *" That to me is what was significant."*

It is interesting to note that Mr. Meredith applied for admission to "Ole Miss" on January 31, 1961. After his application was denied, he sued for admission and his case was appealed until it reached the Supreme Court. The court ruled that James Meredith must be allowed to enroll at the university. In spite of the ruling, Governor Barnett defied the order. There were several conversations between President Kennedy and the Governor. An agreement was finally reached that the Governor would allow Meredith to enroll secretly at the university. The Governor breached the agreement, but if he had kept his word, the "Ole Miss" debacle might have been avoided.

Chief Patrol Inspector Charles Chamblee, second from left, being commended by Ray Ferrell, Commissioner of INS, Attorney General Bobby Kennedy, and James Greene, Associate Commissioner.

Alumni of Ole Miss – Standing, left to right: Charlie Williams, Paul Fullerton, Larry Pinkerton, Ed Klawunn, Lee Erwin, Don Coppock, George Branch, and Bob McCord. Seated, left to right: Gerald Coyle, Bill Randolph, Steve Donnelly, Jim Scoggins, Dave Smith, and James Burns. Photo taken in 2006 at FORBPO conference in Phoenix.

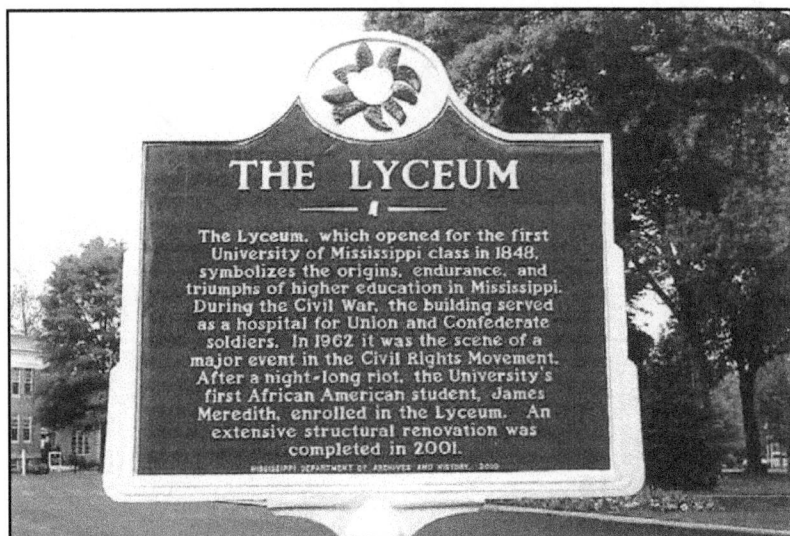

THE LYCEUM

The Lyceum, which opened for the first University of Mississippi class in 1848, symbolizes the origins, endurance, and triumphs of higher education in Mississippi. During the Civil War, the building served as a hospital for Union and Confederate soldiers. In 1962 it was the scene of a major event in the Civil Rights Movement. After a night-long riot, the University's first African American student, James Meredith, enrolled in the Lyceum. An extensive structural renovation was completed in 2001.

MISSISSIPPI DEPARTMENT OF ARCHIVES AND HISTORY, 2010

WASHINGTON

December 6, 1962

Dear Mr. Coppock:

I want to express to you my personal thanks and the thanks of our country for the great service which you rendered on the evening of September 30 in Oxford, Mississippi. Your actions that difficult night were in the highest traditions of the dedicated men and women who serve in law enforcement.

The courage and dedication which you demonstrated while in great personal danger prevented a serious and tragic incident from becoming a disaster for our country. Had you failed, our country would have suffered irreparable damage.

You have my personal gratitude and that of your countrymen.

May I also take this occasion to wish you and your family a happy Christmas.

Sincerely,

John Kennedy

Mr. Donald R. Coppock
Assistant Commissioner, Enforcement
Immigration and Naturalization Service
119 D Street, NE.
Washington 25, D.C.

Office of the Attorney General
Washington, D.C.

Dear Mr. Coppock:

Your praiseworthy actions in assisting other Department of Justice officials in carrying out the court's order affecting the University of Mississippi has come to my attention. Your untiring devotion to duty and coolness under stress had a calming influence on others and contributed greatly to the success of the operation.

It is with a great deal of pleasure that I express my appreciation.

Sincerely,

[signature]
Attorney General

Mr. Donald R. Coppock
Assistant Commissioner, Enforcement
Immigration and Naturalization Service
Washington, D. C.

Congratulations

THE ATTORNEY GENERAL
WASHINGTON

September 2, 1964

Dear Don:

On my last day as Attorney General, I want to thank you for your excellent service to this Department during my tenure.

When we look back four years and see how much was needed to be done, and now how much has been accomplished, you can take great satisfaction in having made an important contribution to the country in a time of maximum need. President Kennedy would have wished to thank you for that--and for your loyalty.

I am proud to have served with you--and I am grateful for your friendship.

With kind regards,

Sincerely,

Robert F. Kennedy

Mr. Donald R. Coppock
Assistant Commissioner
Immigration and Naturalization Service
Department of Justice
Washington, D. C.

A gift from Attorney General Robert Kennedy.

Chapter Six
Bay of Pigs War and the Return of Prisoners to the United States

Early in December of 1962, I was called on to help the Department of Justice in its efforts to bring back to the United States the prisoners that were captured in Cuba during the Bay of Pigs fiasco. In the 1950s a right wing dictator named Fulgencio Batista led Cuba. He dealt with opponents with extreme harshness. While a few prospered under his regime, almost all of the population was very poor. He was not a communist, so he was able to receive support from the United States. His sole support in Cuba came from his army, which was equipped by America. For years Havana, the capital of Cuba, had been the playground of the rich from the United States. They would come to the island on weekends to gamble, and they would spend large sums of money, most of which was skimmed off by Batista. In spite of all the money coming into Cuba, the poor remained poor.

Some of the young Cubans had heard and read about socialism and what it offered the poor, and they reacted against Batista's corruption and his oppression of the downtrodden. Their first attempt to overthrow the government failed, and the small group of rebels fled to the Sierra Mastra, a remote area of Cuba. They sharpened their tactics and used the most valuable weapon they had – educating the poor in their ways. It was only a matter of time before the message spread to other areas of Cuba, and by 1959 the rebels, led by Fidel Castro, felt strong enough to overthrow the Batista government. They easily achieved this feat as they were aided by popular support. After Castro became the dictator of Cuba, many Cubans fled the island and settled mostly in Florida. America reacted by refusing to do any trade with Cuba. This trade embargo would have sent the island into bankruptcy, as Cuba's biggest money earner was the export of sugar to America. Up to that time there was little evidence that Castro had any intensions of doing business with Communist Russia. However, the trade embargo brought the two countries together as Russia stepped in to buy Cuba's sugar and other exports. The actions of America seemed to have driven Castro into the support that was offered by Russia.

Now, with a communist country only fifty miles from the southern tip of Florida, the newly elected American president, John F. Kennedy, decided to give support to the anti-Castro Cubans who had fled to Florida. In 1961 with CIA funding, a group of armed Cuban exiles landed in Cuba at the Bay of Pigs with the sole intention of overthrowing the Cuban government. It proved to be a fiasco. Jeeps landed without fuel; no maps of the island were available; and Cuban exiles fired on Cuban exiles. The invasion of Cuba was a disaster. Additionally, the invasion showed Castro where America stood in relation to Cuba, and he held about thirteen hundred prisoners who had been part of the operation to overthrow his government.

After the Bay of Pigs fiasco, Cuba felt threatened by her powerful neighbor, and Castro started to look for a closer relationship with Russia, a country that would be able to, and capable of, offering Cuba protection. In September 1962, anti-Castro Cuban refugees reported to the CIA that there was a build-up of Russian bases in Cuba. On October 16, 1962, a U2 spy plane took high-level photographs over Cuba that revealed what was obviously a base for missiles, which were later identified as being intermediate range missiles capable of carrying a nuclear payload. On October 17 the CIA reported to the president that sixteen to thirty-two missiles had a range of 2000 miles and could kill up to eighty million Americans. While this was happening, USA intelligence reported that twenty Russian ships were heading for Cuba with crates on board that obviously carried more missiles. They were not difficult to detect, as they were being carried on deck in full view of observer planes. On October 25, 1962, more U2 photographs showed that the bases would be fully operational in a few days, or at the latest by the end of October. The threat to the United States was obvious. On October 27, the matter was made worse when a Russian missile shot down a U2 plane, and the pilot was killed. In total, the Russians sent to Cuba forty-two medium range missiles and twenty-four intermediate missiles. In addition, twenty-two thousand Russian troops and technicians accompanied the missiles. President Kennedy had few choices: he could do nothing; he could order a full-scale invasion of Cuba; he could order an air strike against the missile bases, but this option would result in Russian casualties and the air force was not sure it could deliver pinpoint bombing raids on what were relatively small targets; or, he could call on the Russians to remove the missiles, explaining the damage their presence was doing to Russian/American relations. However, the Russians were highly unlikely to respond to a polite request, since they refused to admit the existence of their missiles at the United Nations emergency meeting about the problem. Also, President Kennedy could put a naval blockade around the island and not allow any more Russian ships to enter Cuba. That would still leave missiles in Cuba, but the negotiations would continue, and President Kennedy would be seen as doing something specific.

President Kennedy chose the fifth option, a naval blockade. Following American protests, Nikita Khrushchev, the Russian leader, sent President Kennedy two letters, both of which sent conflicting messages. One letter stated that the missiles would be withdrawn if Kennedy promised not to invade Cuba. The other was more threatening, claiming that as the USA had bases in Turkey, why couldn't the USSR have bases in Cuba, especially since the people of Cuba wanted them. Khrushchev stated that if the USA removed her missiles from Turkey, then the USSR would remove their missiles from Cuba. President Kennedy decided to act on Khrushchev's first letter. The USSR was to remove its missiles from Cuba, and the USA promised not to invade Cuba. The President was unhappy with the way the CIA had bungled the invasion of Cuba, but he had sympathy for the thirteen hundred prisoners still being held by Castro. The President had discussions with his senior staff members concerning ways to free the prisoners and bring about their return to the United States. It was thought that Castro probably would not deal with the U. S. Government. So, it was decided that James Donovan who lived in New York City, attorney for the Families of Cuban Organizations, would be the best person to deal with the Castro regime. After discussions with the Castro regime, Mr. Donovan reported that Castro would release the prisoners if the American Red Cross would deliver $53,000,000 in food, goods, medicine, pharmaceuticals and drugs to Cuba before Christmas. Of this amount, $42,000,000 worth was to be in baby foods, foods and merchandise, and $11,000,000 was to be in medicines, drugs and pharmaceuticals.

I was detailed to the Department of Justice in early December of 1962 to help accomplish the return of the prisoners. On December 8th a meeting was held in the office of Louis Oberdorfer, Assistant Attorney General for the Tax Division. Present at the meeting were representatives of the Internal Revenue Service, Department of Justice, Central Intelligence Agency, Department of State and myself, as representative of the Border Patrol and the Immigration and Naturalization Service. Although the Red Cross was supposed to be the agency providing the products requested by Mr. Castro, the job was actually accomplished by the United States Government. It was decided that representatives of drug, pharmaceutical, medical, baby food and food companies would be requested to furnish the products that were needed. I was asked to have the Immigration Service make plans to process the prisoners upon their return to the United States. Mr. Oberdorfer told me that we had many things to accomplish in a very short time, and he asked me to prepare a progress chart listing the tasks that needed to be done and the dates they were accomplished. Additionally, companies that produced the products requested by Castro were contacted and asked to meet at the Waldorf Astoria Hotel in New York City to determine what and how much each company would donate. After this was decided, the companies were asked to send a representative to the Department of Justice Building in Washington, D.C. to meet with Internal Revenue Service agents who would, at that time, adjudicate their tax benefits. Participating companies were most anxious to assist President Kennedy, as it was early in his administration and his cause was worthy.

After numerous inquiries and meetings, it was decided that the Opa Locka Airport near Miami, Florida would be used to collect and store less bulky items such as drugs, medicines and pharmaceuticals. We were informed that some of the products, such as plasma and other blood substitutes, were perishable and would need refrigeration. The American Association of Railroads was contacted and they agreed to move a refrigerated car to the Opa Locka Airport. The Air Force furnished a hanger at Opa Locka and agreed to furnish the manpower to unload the products as they arrived. Some of the drugs donated contained narcotics in amounts that came under an international agreement. Accordingly, the companies were requested to identify such drugs so they could be stored separately, as the Bureau of Narcotics informed us that we would need an export license and an import license signed by a representative of the Cuban government. It was determined that the items sent to Opa Locka Airport would be shipped by air to Cuba, and Pan American Airlines was chartered to fly the medicines, drugs, etc., from the Opa Locka Airport and to fly the prisoners back to Homestead Air Force Base, which was located just South of Miami.

The African Pilot, a ship docked at Port Everglades, Florida, was chartered to move the bulky goods and merchandise to Cuba. The companies donating the items to be shipped were requested to send them to Port Everglades by truck or rail. The ship's crew and Port Everglades' stevedores volunteered to unload and load the goods.

As previously stated, James Donovan, attorney for the families of Cubans, was selected to be the contact person and to handle the negotiations with Fidel Castro. Since I was asked to furnish a Border Patrol plane and have it on standby in case it was needed, Border Patrol Pilot Don Harrison flew a Cessna 310 to Washington, D.C. On December 10 pilot Harrison flew to New York City, picked up attorney Donovan, and arrived back in Washington that evening. At approximately 10:00 p.m. that night, the staff at the Justice Department met with Mr. Donovan in Assistant Attorney General Louis Oberdorfer's office and briefed him on the events that had transpired. A letter had been drafted to Mr. Castro informing him of our plans to meet his requests, and attorney Donovan was to hand deliver it to the Cuban leader. Before handing the letter to Donovan, Attorney General Nicholas Katzenbach held the letter up to the light and discovered that embossed in the paper were the words U. S. Government. This was not acceptable since Castro might discover that the U. S. Government was involved and cancel the operation. So late at night, it was difficult to find a store that sold plain paper, but one was found and the letter was retyped. At 1:00 a.m. on December 17th pilot Don Harrison, with attorney James Donovan aboard, departed for Miami, Florida. Harrison later informed me that, during the flight, Donovan would occasionally take sips from small bottles of liquor that he carried in his briefcase. Harrison thought he was probably nervous about his forthcoming meeting with Prime Minister Castro. Upon their arrival in Miami, Mr. Donovan boarded a chartered plane that took him to Cuba.

I was assigned the task of receiving the drugs, medicines and pharmaceuticals at the Opa Locka Airport, where they were to be stored until shipped to Cuba. They were to be stored by category, an inventory kept, and the drugs that had narcotics in them were to be stored separately and guarded twenty-four/seven. E. Barrett Prettyman, an attorney from a prestigious law firm in Washington, was assigned to handle the shipments of the $42,000,000 of the bulkier products that were to be shipped to Cuba.

On December 18th a meeting was held in Attorney General Nicholas Katzenbach's office. Nine of us were present, representing the Immigration Service, the Border Patrol, the State Department, the Air Force, the Justice Department and the Coast Guard. We were seated in a semi-circle around Katzenbach's desk. He opened the meeting by telling us of the importance of our assignments and the necessity of doing our jobs properly in order that the Bay of Pig's prisoners would be returned to the United States. He then asked each of us what our specific assignments were and to explain how they were to be accomplished. Everything went smoothly until he got to Mario Noto, an Associate Commissioner of the Immigration Service who was assigned to receive and process the prisoners upon their return to the United States. To put it as gently as I can, Noto was smart, but not a very popular supervisor. He would have his subordinates prepare a portfolio on problems that were out of the ordinary that would arise. That was his thing. When Katzenbach called upon him, Noto held up a pamphlet and stated that he had a portfolio prepared on the subject. Katzenbach must have known Noto better than I thought, since he replied, *"Noto, I don't give a damn about your portfolio. Tell me how you are going to process the prisoners upon their return to the United States."* Katzenbach also informed us that the prisoners would be returned to Homestead Air Force Base since they had the facilities we needed.

At 2:45 p.m. on December 19th, attorney Prettyman and I departed Washington in the Border Patrol plane, arriving at the Opa Locka Airport at 8:00 p.m. The following day we arranged to have several phones installed in hangar 102 at the airport and at the Port Everglades terminal; these phones were to be manned twenty-four/ seven. Pilot Harrison and I were the only officers at Opa Locka, and I couldn't get help from the Miami Border Patrol Sector as Noto had them all assigned to his operation. Consequently, I had two officers detailed to my operation from the New Orleans Sector. Since planes were needed for the shipment of goods to Cuba and the return of the prisoners, I completed these arrangements with Mr. William Raven, division manager of Pan American Airways.

Planeloads of cargo started arriving at Opa Locka on the December 21st, and we were kept busy storing the drugs by category, separating those that contained narcotics, and keeping the inventory. Representatives of the Red Cross were present and they immediately started making and receiving calls on our phones. My help complained that they were unable to do their jobs as the Red Cross had all of the phones tied up. I talked to the Red Cross supervisor and told him that we needed to use the phones, and from henceforth they could use only one telephone. About an hour later I received a call from Attorney General Katzenbach telling me that he had received a call from the Red Cross complaining that I wouldn't let them use the phones; he asked for me to try and placate them, which I did, of course. At approximately 2:00 a.m., representatives of the Cuban Red Cross and Cuban officials arrived at Opa Locka to inspect the materials stored there. All of my officers had to vacate the premises in order to make it appear that the Red Cross was handling the operation. The Cubans departed Miami International Airport for Cuba at 9:30

a.m. that morning. The Bureau of Narcotics kept reminding me that in addition to the export license for the drugs with narcotics, they needed an import license signed by a representative of the Cuban government before he could release the drugs for shipment. I informed him that I would give the application to the pilot of the first plane that departed for Cuba. The ship, African Pilot, loaded with the materials requested by Castro departed Port Everglades at 9:40 a.m. on December 22nd. At 6:00 a.m. on December 24th, I called Mr. Katzenbach at his home and informed him that we were ready to start the airlift. As he had no further instructions, the first plane departed for Cuba at 6:10 a.m. At approximately 10:00 a.m. the plane returned from Cuba and by telephone the crew was debriefed by Mr. Oberdorfer. Everything seemed to be going smoothly, however he didn't have the signed import license. The last two planes departed for Cuba on the morning of the 24th. Later that day pilot Harrison and I flew to Homestead Air Force Base to await the return of the prisoners. That evening the prisoners started arriving, and by 9:30 p.m. they had all been returned to the United States. There was a feeling of elation that the operation was over and that it had gone so well. However, the signed import license was not received. I later learned that it was given to the Captain of the African Pilot, and upon its return to Port Everglades on December 26th it was given to the Bureau of Narcotics. The narcotics agent I dealt with at Opa Locks was a nice looking and clean-cut person, and we became well acquainted. He told me that he would be testifying before the House Budget Committee in a couple of weeks, and he asked me to attend if I could. I was able to attend the hearing, and after it was over we visited for a short time before I returned to my office. A few weeks later I read in the paper that he had been arrested and charged for taking a four hundred dollar a month bribe from a drug dealer.

After the prisoners arrived, the commanding general in charge of Homestead Air Force Base had a cocktail party for those of us who had been involved in the operation. Noto and his principal helper, Bob Schoenenberger, were not invited, so I asked Mr. Oberdorfer to request the General to invite them, which he did. During the party the General told us that he had a Jet Star plane standing by to return us to Washington after the party was over. Mr. Oberdorfer asked me to furnish Border Patrol vehicles to take us to the plane and requested that I keep it as quiet as possible. I relayed the request to Mr. Schoenenberger, as Noto had all of the vehicles assigned to his operation. Schoenenberger lost it! He went into a rage, cursing and saying that he wouldn't keep it quiet, and indicating they would not furnish the cars for us. I replied that that was fine, and I would arrange for the Air Force to furnish the transportation. He then cooled down and agreed to furnish the vehicles. We arrived in Washington around 1:00 a.m. on Christmas morning, and the Air Force furnished cars that took each of us to our homes. They were most hospitable, and are to be commended for their help.

On the evening of December 28th, my wife Shirley and I were sitting in our den at home when I got a call from Mr. Oberdorfer at about 10:00 p.m. telling us that we were invited to fly to Miami the following morning in an Air Force plane to attend President Kennedy's speech to the Cuban prisoners. He also stated that the plane would depart Washington National Airport at 6:00 a.m., and he then asked me to furnish Border Patrol Vehicles to transport the nineteen people that would be on the flight from the airport to the Orange Bowl. The plane had a strong head wind and when we arrived at the Orange Bowl the President was already speaking. We sat in the end zone until the speech was over, and as the President and Mrs. Kennedy were leaving in an open-air car, he stopped and came up to our seats in the bleachers and talked with Mr. Oberdorfer and myself. The President was most hospitable and thanked us for the work we had done. He and Mrs. Kennedy were very impressive and a most handsome couple. Once again, the Border Patrol had participated in and been of great help in a major event in the history of our country.

E. Barrett Prettyman and I standing in front of PROGRESS REPORT board with three other Department of Justice officials.

HOGAN & HARTSON

COLORADO BUILDING

WASHINGTON 5, D. C.

TELEPHONE
STerling 3-1906

CABLE ADDRESS
"HOGANDER WASHINGTON"

January 3, 1963

Honorable Donald R. Coppock
Assistant Commissioner, Enforcement
Immigration and Naturalization Service
119 D Street, N. E.
Washington, D. C.

Dear Don:

I hope I can somehow express my great appreciation for
the tremendous job you did during the recent Cuban prisoner
exchange. Without fuss (and often without sleep), you constantly came up with the right answer at the right time. You
never once failed the group, and you were often three steps
ahead of us in seeing that things were done that had to be
done.

This job simply could not have been accomplished without you, and I, for one, want you to know that I feel deeply
indebted to you for the part you played. Even more importantly,
I feel that I made a good personal friend.

My best to your wife and family and every good wish
for the new year.

Sincerely yours,

E. Barrett Prettyman, Jr.

EBP:jlb

cc: Honorable Raymond F. Farrell

LFO:meg

December 31, 1962

Honorable Raymond F. Farrell
Commissioner
Immigration & Naturalization Service
Washington 25, D. C.

Dear Ray:

As I told you over the phone the other day,
you should know that you have a rare prize in Don Coppock.
In the recent Cuban operation, both here in Washington
and in Miami, Don proved again what a calm and effective
worker and leader he is. As I told him and you, any time
I have anything to do with a tough operation, I want Don
in it.

Many thanks for allowing him to work with us
again.

Best regards.

Sincerely,

(Signed) Lou

Louis F. Oberdorfer
Assistant Attorney General

bcc: Attorney General
Deputy Attorney General
Mr. Donald R. Coppock

Chapter Seven
Civil Strife and Bombings in Birmingham, Alabama

In May of 1963 there were severe racial riots in Birmingham, Alabama. Groups of Negroes attempting to pursue their civil rights were rioting and clashing with the police. Eugene "Bull" Connor, Commissioner of Police and a well-known fanatical segregationist, was brutal in attempting to control the situation. His police were using firemen's high-pressure water hoses, dogs and nightsticks against the Negroes. Pictures of these clashes were on the television news every day, and it was apparent that strong and decisive action was needed to alleviate the situation.

On May 12th Deputy Attorney General Nicholas Katzenbach called Assistant Attorney General Louis Oberdorfer and directed him to proceed to Birmingham aboard an Air Force plane that was to depart Andrews Air Force Base as soon after 1:00 p.m. as possible. The group included Ramsey Clark, John Dolan, John Nolan, James Malley of the FBI and me. We assembled at the Department of Justice where we were briefed on the situation and arrangements made for the FBI to meet us in Birmingham. After arriving at the airport, we proceeded to the FBI headquarters on Eighth Avenue. United States

Attorney Macon Weaver met us there. We learned that Martin Luther King, Jr. was scheduled to arrive in Birmingham at 3:30 p.m., and he was going directly downtown where the confrontations were occurring. Mr. King tried several strategies in trying to alleviate the situation, but to no avail. He finally was jailed on a civil disobedience charge. Assistant Attorney General Burke Marshall called and asked us to make an evaluation of the situation after Mr. King's arrival. Not much had changed. The State Highway Patrol Officers had withdrawn from the Birmingham area without any notice to the Sheriff or Police Department. A little while later a large meeting of the Ku Klux Klan was held near Bessemer, Alabama, with approximately five thousand Klan members attending. Soon after the Klan meeting, there were bombings at the home of Reverend A. D. King and at the Gaston Motel where Martin Luther King had been living. These bombings provoked a violent reaction from the Negroes. They rioted and, due to the seriousness of the situation, the Highway Patrol Officers returned hastily, using the butts of their rifles and shotguns, along with their billy clubs and, with the help of the city police, quelled the riot after it had raged for a substantial period of time. In view of the tactics used there were serious and extensive injuries. During the riot fires broke out in the area, and the rioters prevented firemen from reaching the fires until the police escorted them into the area. President Kennedy had the Army on stand-by in case they were needed. The Army had a two-hour response time, and because of the increasing seriousness of the situation, was moved to Fort McClellan, a closer site from which they could respond more rapidly, if they were needed. One of my assignments was to establish liaison with the police department and let them know that we were there to help and to learn what I could about their strategies and intentions. I was in a car with a supervisory police officer at a location where the police had gathered, and as we were talking "Bull" Connor arrived on the scene. When the officer I was with saw Mr. Connor, he asked me to move because he didn't want "Bull" to see him with me.

We were asked to make a survey of the seriousness of the situation for the Attorney General so he could make a recommendation to the President as to whether the Army was needed. U. S. Attorney Macon Weaver loaned Colonel Keller civilian clothes so that he could mix in with the crowd and make the determination concerning the necessity for the Army. At the time, planes with soldiers aboard were flying over Birmingham, but they were not to land without orders from the President. Colonel Keller stated that troops were not needed at that time.

Mr. Oberdorfer placed a telephone call to the Chief of Police, Jaime Moore, and to the Sheriff, Melvin Bailey, inviting them to the FBI Office to discuss the situation. Both agreed to meet with the Federal officials. Chief Moore arrived first. His lack of sleep and pure exhaustion showed in his eyes and the drawn lines of his face. When it was made clear to Chief Moore that troops would be used if it became necessary, he seemed glad to hear it. When asked if his officers would cooperate should troops be moved in, he replied 100% in the affirmative. He then said, *"I don't know what 'Bull's' group will do."* He then added, *"If Connor stays in office, I am going to resign, as I can't take it anymore."* Sheriff Melvin Bailey soon joined the group, and he stated flatly that he was glad we were there, and that he and his deputies would cooperate fully. Both the Chief of Police and the Sheriff said that they thought they had the situation under control unless more trouble broke out.

On May 14, while waiting in the U. S. Marshall's Office, I had a most unusual and interesting conversation with Chief Deputy U. S. Marshall Dan Moore. As I visited with Mr. Moore I asked him how the situation looked, and he replied that everything seemed okay, and if the people from Washington and up North would go home, things would sort themselves out. He further stated that, "Those people from the North don't practice what they preach, and until they do they shouldn't be trying to force integration on the folks in the South." I asked him what he meant, and he replied that he had worked in Washington in the Attorney General's Office, and he didn't see anyone up there taking Negroes home to dinner, or white children running around with Negroes like they are trying to make us do. I immediately excused myself after learning of his attitude, so that I wouldn't have to listen to such a diatribe. I mentioned the conversation to Chief U. S. Marshall Norville, and he told me that Moore was an acquaintance and follower of Governor George Wallace. The situation improved, the Army was not used, and I returned to Washington on Friday, May 17th.

On Sunday, September 15, 1963, my wife Shirley

and I returned home from church about 12:20 p.m. The phone was ringing; it was a call from the Department of Justice. I was informed that there had been a bombing in Birmingham, Alabama, killing four young colored girls. I was told to be at Andrews Air Force Base by 1:30 p.m. and that an Air Force plane would be waiting to take our party to Birmingham. Attorney General Ramsey Clark was in charge of the detail; upon arrival in Birmingham, we were furnished an office in the Federal Courthouse. It was learned on the morning of September 15th a white man was seen placing a box under the steps of the Sixteenth Street Baptist Church. Soon afterwards, at 10:22 a.m., the bomb exploded killing Denise McNair, age eleven; Addie Mae Collins, age fourteen; Carole Robertson, age fourteen; and Cynthia Wesley, age fourteen. The girls had been attending Sunday school classes at the church. There were also twenty-three other people injured during the explosion.

The Sixteenth Street Baptist Church was used as a meeting place for civil rights leaders such as Martin Luther King Jr., Ralph Abernathy and Fred Shutterworth. Racial tensions increased dramatically when these leaders and others became involved in a campaign to register African Americans to vote in Birmingham. This was the 21st bombing in Birmingham over an eight-year period, and the first bombing in which anyone was killed. Birmingham had become known as "Bombingham". The bombing was such a dastardly act that the Governor, George Wallace, condemned it. The city of Birmingham offered a $52,000 reward, and the Governor offered another $5,000 if the bombers were apprehended. Martin Luther King Jr. notified President Kennedy that he was going to Birmingham to plead with the Negroes to remain non-violent. The Sixteenth Street Baptist Church bombing was a galvanizing moment in the civil rights movement. Moderates who had stayed on the sidelines could no longer remain silent, and the fight to topple segregation gained new momentum. On September 15th, Martin Luther King conducted the funeral service for three of the little girls, during which he stated, *"These children – unoffending, innocent and beautiful – were the victims of one of the most vicious and tragic crimes perpetrated against humanity."*

After an investigation that lasted a year and a half, on May 13, 1965 a memorandum notified J. Edgar Hoover that the bombing was the work of former Klu Klux Klansmen Robert "Bomber" Chambliss, Bobby Cherry, Herman Cash and Thomas Blanton, Jr. It took years to bring these creeps to justice. On November 18, 1977, Chambliss was convicted on a state murder charge and sentenced to life in prison. He died in prison still professing his innocence in the bombing. Cash died in February of 1977. On May 17, 2000, Blanton and Cherry surrendered on murder indictments returned by a grand jury in Birmingham. In 2001, the judge delayed Cherry's trial citing the defendant's medical problems. On May 1, 2001, Blanton was convicted for his part in the bombing.

While in Birmingham we again met with the Chief of Police, Jamie Moore, and other officials concerning the bombing and other civil rights issues. After our discussions we were convinced that they would try to solve the bombing case, and would work to ameliorate civil strife in the area. About midnight on the night before we were to return home, I was sitting in the office visiting with Ramsey Clark, the Attorney General, and I remember him telling me that he was going to Tulsa the next day. He told me that Senator Kerr from Oklahoma had sponsored a bill that would make the Arkansas River navigable from Tulsa to the Mississippi River, and would benefit Oklahoma for a hundred years or more. This was the first time that I became well acquainted with Mr. Clark. I also recall him telling me that the poor and downtrodden should not only be able to demonstrate and protest, but that they should be given a forum to express their views and problems. This may have been an indication of his bizarre actions later in his life. During the years I knew and dealt with him, he was a strong supporter of law and order, and he was a friend who treated me exceptionally well.

Chapter Eight
Termination of the Bracero Program and Increase of Illegal Entries

On December 31, 1964, the Bracero Program, which went into effect during World War II and permitted growers to contract Mexican laborers who were guaranteed a specific wage, was terminated as a result of pressure from the labor unions. The incidence of entry without inspection on the Mexican border had been running slightly over thirty thousand to almost forty-five thousand annually. A very acceptable number when compared to the number of illegal aliens that had been apprehended in recent years. We knew that the number of Mexican illegal entries would increase, and the question arose as to what we should do about it. I discussed the situation with my staff, and we decided that we should attempt to do something to deter their employment. As a result, we wrote proposed legislation that would make it a violation to knowingly hire an alien who was in the United States illegally. The proposed legislation also provided for a $1,000 fine for each illegal alien employed. It also provided that the grower complete a form I-9 for each person hired, and if the person presented a social security card or a driver's license, the employer would not be held liable. This proposed legislation was pigeonholed in the Commissioner's office for several years. The primary mission of the Border Patrol is to prevent the smuggling and unlawful entry of aliens into the United States, and to apprehend persons guilty of such violations. This proposed legislation was a first step to fulfill and enforce our mission. As expected, illegal entry of Mexican aliens increased dramatically, from slightly over thirty thousand in 1965 to over one hundred and twenty thousand in 1968. At that time, the Department of Justice asked the Immigration Service to prepare legislation that would make it a violation to hire an alien that was illegally in the United States. The legislation that we had prepared years earlier was dusted off and sent to the Department. The Department approved of the draft, and forwarded it to the legislature, where it was enacted into law. The enforcement of this statute helped, but the illegal entry of Mexican aliens continued to increase, and it became evident that additional enforcement efforts were needed to combat the problem. The Vietnam War was being fought, and I had read that the Army was using sensors to detect North Vietnamese soldiers who were going south on the Ho Chi Minh Trail. The trail was named after the President of North Vietnam. Realizing that sensors could be adapted to detect the illegal entry of aliens crossing our borders, I pondered what to do about it. Knowing that it would take years to procure sensors through the normal budget process, I thought about possibly obtaining some from the Army. Not knowing whom to contact at the Department of Defense, I thought of a friend, who was in the Army and that I had gone to school with in Cherokee, Oklahoma. He had been in the National Guard in Oklahoma, had served in World War II, and was now Inspector General of the Army and had his office in the Pentagon. I called General Garrison, and after exchanging pleasantries, I explained to him the reason for my call. He suggested that I have lunch with him the next day at the Pentagon so we could discuss the matter further. I took a member of my staff, Richard Wischkaemper with me, as he was more knowledgeable than I was about sensor bytes, radio frequencies, etc. After expressing our needs and interest in the use of sensors to aid in our mission, General Garrison put me in touch with the person in charge of the sensor operations for the Army. After we told him what we needed, he informed me that the Army had some surplus sensors that he would donate to the Border Patrol. He also told me that he would like to work with us since he would like to test the future generations of sensors along our borders as to their reliability. Of course I was delighted to accept his offer.

After the military sensors were placed in the Chula Vista Sector, I suggested that they keep a record of the number of aliens detected and apprehended by each sensor. I met with some resistance on that part of the project, but after explaining the importance of the figures requested in order to justify the request for funds to purchase additional sensors, it was agreed that the statistics needed would be furnished. Shortly after the partial system was installed in the Chula Vista Sector, a reporter from the San Diego Times-Union interviewed the Deputy Chief, Richard Batchelor. Mr. Batchelor stated:

> In my 30 years of experience this present system of electronic intrusion detection is the most successful step the Border Patrol has ever taken. We have increased our capabilities without having to increase our manpower. The Sensor System is like a middle line backer on a football team. It allows the agent to sit back and watch the play develop, then he can rush to the hole and plug up the gap by himself. The sensors give the Border Patrol 20th Century capabilities when we need them to stop illegal entries all along our borders.

The early remotely monitored sensor system we used was based on sensors using the seismic disturbance principal of detection. Because of the nature of seismic detection, it reacts to other than man or vehicle induced seismic noise, such as over-flying aircraft, thunder, high winds and various other phenomena. Accordingly, in many areas we would place an additional sensor on a trail in order to verify an intrusion over our borders, and to decide whether it was a "go" or "no go" for an officer to respond. After the skeleton sensor system was installed in the Chula Vista Sector, we found that the results far exceeded expectations, and a determination was made to expand the system in Chula Vista, and to acquire and install systems in the El Paso, Del Rio, Tucson and Yuma Sectors as rapidly as budget and engineering limitations permitted. In spite of the above-described actions, the illegal entry of Mexican aliens continued to increase. Please remember the earlier discussion of the success of the "bus lift" from El Paso to

Ojinaga, Chihuahua, Mexico, and the "train lift" from there to Chihuahua City in 1953. Also, there was the success of the so called "Wetback Drive" in 1954, when approximately eight hundred Border Patrol Inspectors and Investigators were detailed to the Western part of the United States to rid the area of illegal Mexican aliens. Adult male Mexican aliens when apprehended were sent to a detention center in El Centro, California. From there they were bussed to Nogales, Sonora, Mexico where they were placed on trains, and at the expense of the Mexican government, transported to the interior of Mexico. After about forty-five days, the operation was shifted to South Texas where adult Mexican aliens were boatlifted from Port Isabel, Texas to Vera Cruz and Tapioca, Mexico. In addition, the Border Patrol had acquired six DC-6 transport airplanes, and European and other foreign aliens who were apprehended were flown back to their native countries.

Almost all aliens, especially Mexican aliens, enter the United States to improve their economic status. If you take the profit out of their illegal entry, they will not come; they will find it better to stay home. You do this by sending adult male Mexican aliens who are from the interior of Mexico or who are repeating offenders to a port of entry several hundred miles from the border. Juvenile and women repeat offenders were returned to Mexico at a port of entry some ten to twenty miles from their homes. As previously mentioned, after the Bracero Program was terminated in 1964, the illegal entry of Mexican aliens continued to increase. To counter this invasion we started bus, train and airlifts of adult Mexican aliens to the interior of the country. Chief Patrol Inspector Alan Gerhardt in Chula Vista, California, negotiated a contract with a Mexican charter service to fly adult male Mexicans from Tijuana to Leon, Gto, Mexico. This was by far the most effective "lifts" program that we had. As I recall, the plane had a capacity to seat one hundred and twenty aliens, and the fare charged was only $30 per alien. I don't suppose we could do it now, but at that time we gave each alien a choice – pay the $30 fare or be prosecuted. Almost all of the aliens choose to pay the fare. We had a policy of leaving the alien with at least $20, and if he couldn't pay the full fare we would issue a travel voucher to cover the balance. The Tijuana Airport was adjacent to the international border, and a gate was built into the fence. At 11:00 p.m. each night one hundred and twenty aliens would be taken across the border to the waiting plane, which would fly them to Leon, Gto, Mexico. This airlift was a very effective operation since it drastically reduced illegal entries in the sector. However, after a few months, the Commissioner of the Immigration Service and a couple of his aides made a trip to Mexico City, and upon their return, I was instructed to terminate the airlift immediately. I was not told the reason for this, but I feel positive it was a political decision.

Between 1964, the year the Bracero Program was terminated, and 1972, several steps were taken to deter the illegal entry of aliens, especially Mexicans, since over 95% of the aliens apprehended were from Mexico. A new program required that copies of the apprehension reports of Mexican aliens caught in the interior be sent to the sector through which the alien entered, pinpointing the place of entry as nearly as possible. Sixty-two Border Patrol positions were transferred from the Canadian to the Mexican border. Additionally, the following bus/train lifts were initiated, and undercover Mexican officers and informants would ride the lifts occasionally to assure that aliens remained on the lifts until they reached their destination:

El Paso - Presidio/Ojinaga and then train
to Chihuahua, Mexico
El Paso - Jimeniz, Mexico
El Paso - Chihuahua, Mexico
Port Isabel - San Luis Potosi, Mexico
El Centro - Mazatlan, Mexico
El Centro - Obregon, Mexico
Chula Vista - Mazatlan, Mexico
Del Rio - San Luis Potosi, Mexico
Nogales - Mazatlan, Mexico
Nogales - Obregon, Mexico

These lifts were not as effective as the previous airlift. The authorized force of the Border Patrol increased from 1,493 in 1964 to 1,695 in 1972, and the apprehension of Mexican aliens increased during this period from slightly over 35,000 to 355,000. In 1996 the Border Patrol retiree organization, the Fraternal Order of Retired Border Patrol Officers, had their annual conference in El Paso. The newly selected Chief of the Border Patrol was in attendance, and I asked him to have breakfast with me. During the meal, I told him that I didn't want to seem presumptuous, and I suggested to him that to control the illegal entry of Mexican aliens, he would have to take the profit out of their coming to the United States to work, and to do that he would have to return them to the interior of Mexico under the conditions that I have previously described. He replied, *"Don, with the increase in manpower and new techniques, I'll be able to control the border."* How misguided he was. As I write this in 2006, there are an estimated twelve million illegal aliens in the United States, and the number is growing. Congress is debating a bill that would add an additional 700 miles of fencing. This would help, but it is not a complete answer to the problem. In addition to removing Mexican aliens to the interior of their country, the government should enforce laws that are presently in effect, and fine employers who hire illegal aliens $1,000 for each illegal employee who is apprehended. This would certainly help in getting the situation under control.

Chapter Nine
Work in the 1960s

Throughout the 1960's I was involved in one additional major civil rights demonstration and several smaller ones. During this period, my wife Shirley and I were fortunate to enjoy an interesting social life. There is one such event that I recall vividly. We were invited to a cocktail party on Capital Hill that was hosted by an Oklahoma Congressman. Shirley was teaching school, and I asked her to ride the train from Riverdale, Maryland to Washington, D.C. where I would meet her and we could then go to the party together. After the party, we arrived at our home in my car, and then realized that we had left Shirley's car at the train station. On the way to the station I took an unfamiliar route. Trees were in full bloom and leaves blocked the view of a stop sign. I saw the sign just as I went through the intersection, and there was a policeman sitting in his cruiser on the side street. He, of course, stopped me and as he was looking at my car's registration and my driver's license, I told him that I was employed in law enforcement. He replied, *"Why didn't you tell me?"* and he closed his ticket book, said for us to have a nice day and got in his car. I had just started wearing eyeglasses, and I didn't have them; I suppose because I was a little vain. Not being able to see clearly up close, I put the car in reverse instead of drive and backed into the policeman's car. I didn't hit him hard, but he came up to me and said, *"You had better let your wife drive,"* which I gladly did.

During John Kennedy's presidency we were invited to a reception at the White House. As he and Mrs. Kennedy came down the spiral staircase (he in a tuxedo and she in an exquisite evening dress), the Marine Corps Band was softly playing "Hail to the Chief". It was truly an exhilarating moment! As they entered the room, the President came directly to Shirley and shook her hand, perhaps because she looked a little Irish to him. The Kennedy's were a very striking and handsome couple. After President Kennedy was assassinated, President Johnson appointed Ramsey Clark as his Attorney General. Ramsey's father, Tom Clark, was a member of the Supreme Court, and he retired so there would not be a conflict of interest. Shirley and I attended a reception at the Supreme Court Building. (See photo of me talking to Ramsey and Tom Clark at reception) While we were having this conversation, Tom Clark told me the following story. During the year that President Truman was running for President, Tom was in El Paso, Texas, and he and Grover Wilmouth, District Director of the Immigration Service in El Paso, were driven to Lordsburg, New Mexico, where they met the President who was on a whistle stop train campaign. Between Lordsburg and El Paso, they discussed ways that he could gain votes in the El Paso area and all along the Mexican border. There were always tensions between growers and the Border Patrol since the Patrol was continuously apprehending aliens employed by the growers. During the trip the President and his aides devised a plan that the Border Patrol could not check laborers on farms without a warrant and that we could only apprehend aliens who were in the act of entering the United States or were on public lands. I remembered when that happened, but this was the first I had heard of the details and the reason for the order.

In 1965 I was president of the Oklahoma State Society in Washington, D.C. During my tenure, Carl Albert, an Oklahoma Congressman, was selected to be majority leader of the House of Representatives. While at a meeting with other officials of the Society, we decided to have a party to celebrate Mr. Albert's promotion. It was my thought that the party would be for members of the Oklahoma State Society, members of the Oklahoma delegation and congressional officials. I appointed J. D. Williams, head of a Washington law firm, as the finance chairman for the occasion. Mr. Williams had previously been on Senator Bob Kerr's staff, and while working there he got his Masters Degree in tax law and was now a well-known lobbyist and a good friend. When he first started practicing law, he had some immigrant clients, and he would come to my office occasionally so I could refer him to the person with whom he needed to speak. He was struggling at the time; his wife Carol taught school and they lived in an apartment. He was an extremely bright individual, and it certainly paid off for him. A year or two after that, Shirley and I were invited to a party he was giving, honoring the Attorney General from Oklahoma, at his new house in Virginia. We found his street all right, but we had a hard time locating his house. We finally found a driveway that led to his residence. The driveway crossed a brook, and his lovely home was situated on several acres of land. It was a very beautiful estate.

A few years after I retired, Shirley and I were in Kiowa, Kansas at a Labor Day function. We were eating our lunch, which was on plates we held on our laps. As I was eating I noticed a man standing in front of me, and as I looked up I recognized that it was Bob Dole who was running for reelection to the Senate. After we visited a few minutes, I told him that we had a mutual friend in Washington. He, of course, asked whom, and I told him it was J. D. Williams. Mr. Dole replied that J. D. was really very busy. I asked doing what, and he gestured with his hands, and said, "Counting his money. One million, two million, three million,...."

Getting back to the party for Mr. Albert, who was known as the "Giant of Little Dixie" in Oklahoma, J. D., the Chairman of finances for the occasion, invited all the members of the House of Representatives, members of the Senate, members of the Supreme Court and the President and Mrs. Johnson, as well as senior members of his staff. When I heard of this I was dumbfounded. The Society didn't have the money to fund such an occasion, so I called a meeting on a Sunday afternoon in the Shrine building of the Oklahoma State Society officials. I opened the meeting by telling J. D. that we did not have the funds to pay for all the people he had invited, and he replied, "Don, if we are going to have this affair, we are going to do it right. I will take care of raising the money for the party. The party was held in the Sheraton Park Hotel, and it was attended by hundreds of Mr. Albert's friends and associates. I was able to get the late Frank McGee (anchor man for NBC News in New York City and originally from Norman, Oklahoma) to come down from New York and be the Master of Ceremonies. I introduced Mr. McGee. He gave a speech and showed photographs of the school Mr. Albert attended at Bug Tussle, Oklahoma, and many events of his earlier years were shown on a large screen. The President and his entourage were in attendance at the affair. The evening was a huge success, and when everything was paid for, we had a profit of over $5,000. I got a good lesson in "Politics 101", and the old story that MONEY IS THE MOTHER'S MILK OF POLITICS seems to be true.

During the 1960's, regional and sector chiefs would occasionally be detailed to the central office for conferences, and quite often I would call Shirley and tell her that I was bringing from five to eight officers home for dinner. Although she was teaching, she always rose to the occasion, and we would cook steaks or hamburgers on the grill, and, of course, always enjoyed their company. I was blessed to have a very competent staff. Robert Stewart was my deputy, and I would normally confer with him about new ideas and strategies; and he didn't hesitate to tell me if he thought I was wrong. I was honored to give the eulogy at his funeral. Most of my sector chiefs were outstanding leaders, and they certainly contributed to any success that I may have achieved.

One very beneficial thing I did in the 1960's was to become involved in the Big Brothers Program. I was a big brother to Greg Gordon, a young man from a fatherless family. I would occasionally take him to the Washington Senators baseball games, but he really wasn't that interested. He was more interested in eating hotdogs and popcorn. We would often have him over to our house for cookouts and sunday dinners. It was a worthwhile effort as he earned a college degree and is gainfully employed.

A personal matter that occurred in the '60's may be of interest. In 1959 our daughter Mary-Blue attended Colorado College in Colorado Springs, Colorado. It was her first year of college and the first time that she had been away from Shirley and me, and she was terribly homesick. We gritted our teeth and made her stay the full year. She got over her homesickness, and at the end of the school year she called and asked if she could stay and visit a friend for a few days. The next year she attended Maryland University, which was located about a mile from our house. I think I saw her more often when she was in Colorado than I did when she was in Maryland. Shirley and I had told Mary-Blue that if she ever needed us for anything to call, no matter what time of the day it was. While attending Maryland University, we got a call from her at about 12:30 a.m. one night telling us that she and two of her sorority sisters were at a house in Silver Springs, Maryland with three boys who wouldn't take them home. I don't recall how she knew the address but she did, and we told her that we would be there as soon as possible. We located the address, and I walked in without knocking, pushed one of the boys against the wall, and stated that I didn't appreciate this a g– d— bit and told the girls to get in the car. Mary-Blue took a lot of ribbing from her sorority sisters about her protective parents.

Visiting with Attorney General Ramsey Clark and his father, Associate Justice of the Supreme Court Tom Clark, at a reception in Supreme Court building.

Congress of the United States
House of Representatives
Office of the Majority Leader
Washington, D.C.

August 2, 1966

Mr. Donald Coppock, President
Oklahoma State Society
4419 Underwood Street
University Park, Maryland

Dear Don:

Well, you did it again!

You have really made this an "Albert Year" for the Oklahoma
State Society.

We can't begin to thank you enough for Friday evening. It
was one of those near-perfect occasions. Mary, Mary Frances,
David and I are all deeply grateful to you, the Oklahoma
Society, the University of Oklahoma and the Oklahoma State
University Alumni Associations, and all those who had a
hand in making it a success.

Our best wishes always.

Sincerely,

CARL ALBERT, M. C.
Third District, Oklahoma

CA/Whn

Photo of Chief Patrol Inspectors during a conference at Port Isabel, Texas, during the 1960s.

Introducing Speaker of the House of Representative Carl Albert at an Oklahoma State Society meeting.

LAW OFFICES OF

SUTHERLAND, ASBILL & BRENNAN

WASHINGTON

August 1, 1966

Mr. Donald R. Coppock
4419 Underwood Street
University Park, Maryland

Dear Don:

I thought the Carl Albert Dinner was a splendid grand finale for your year as President of the Oklahoma State Society, which I feel will go down in Society history as the best to date. You did an especially good job in handling your speaking assignments at the Dinner last Friday and I think that, on the whole, you have been too modest about your contribution to the success of the Society during the last year. You deserve everyone's gratitude if for no other reason than for being able to assemble and hold together the workers it takes to give such events as the Congressional Reception, the Cherry Blossom Princess Ball, and the Albert Dinner.

I certainly enjoyed working with you and am grateful for the confidence which you displayed in me over the last year.

With every good wish, I am

Sincerely,

J. D. Williams

JDW:mab

Chapter Ten
The Selma to Montgomery, Alabama March

As I mentioned earlier, I was involved in one other major civil rights demonstration and a few minor ones in the 1960's. In mid-March of 1965, I attended a meeting in the Attorney General's Office. He informed those present that the Negroes and other civil rights activists were planning a march from Selma to Montgomery, Alabama, and that the march was scheduled to begin on Friday, March 19th and end on Wednesday, March 24th. During the meeting, he informed me that he had several tasks for the Border Patrol and me. He requested that the Border Patrol furnish radio communications from the command center in Montgomery to Selma, so that he could stay in touch with the progress of the marchers and those officers protecting them. He also asked me to go to Montgomery prior to the beginning of the march and talk to the Governor or his representative to urge and determine if the Governor would call up the National Guard to protect the marchers. He asked, also, that I be prepared to furnish Border Patrol officers if the National Guard was not activated. Additionally, he asked me to rent an office that would have a view of the marchers' arrival at the capital and to have a telephone installed.

I had Chief Patrol Inspector Charles Chamblee and a radio technician from New Orleans meet me in Montgomery. I asked the radio technician to establish radio communications from the base station in Montgomery to Selma, a distance of about fifty miles. He drove to Selma, and when he returned, he informed me that to furnish the radio communications requested he would have to put a repeater on an AT&T tower, as there was no other place available. I called the local AT&T representative, and he told me that the company had a policy not to permit anyone to place anything on their towers, and that he could not permit us to use the tower. I then called the district representative, and he told me the same thing, and stated that perhaps I might call their regional office. I called the regional office and I was again told that we couldn't place a repeater on their tower. Then I called assistant Attorney General Louis Oberdorfer, and I explained the situation to him and suggested that someone might contact the corporate office in New York. In just a short while, the local representative in Montgomery got a call telling him to let us put a repeater on their tower. I never knew who contacted the corporate office, but it certainly got results. The next day the district representative called me asking me if we had installed our repeater on the tower. When I replied in the affirmative, he asked that I please call the regional office and tell them that we were on the tower, as the regional rep had been bugging him about the matter. I, of course, did so. That same day I met with Willie B. Painter, Captain of the Alabama Public Safety and the Governor's representative about calling up the National Guard to protect the marchers. During the meeting, he stated that he had reservations about the National Guard's ability to adequately protect the marchers, and after a long discussion, we agreed to meet again the next morning. After this meeting, it became clear that the Governor was not going to call up the National Guard, but Painter suggested that we might want to federalize them. This was really no surprise, as the Governor at that time was a strong segregationist.

The next evening I met Attorney General Ramsey Clark and Department of Justice Public Relations Officer Jack Rosenthal, who had flown in from Washington. As we left the airport, the Attorney General asked me about the outcome of my meetings relating to the Governor calling up the National Guard to protect the marchers. I replied that we had a *"Mexican standoff."* Mr. Clark understood the statement, but Jack asked, "*What in the world is a 'Mexican standoff'?*" I explained that the meetings had been cordial and friendly, but in the end the Governor was not going to call up the Guard. The Attorney General requested that I furnish Border Patrol Officers to guard the marchers. Accordingly, thirty officers were detailed from the Miami and New Orleans Sectors to the operation, along with fifteen unmarked, radio equipped vehicles. I had asked Chief Chamblee to select a Patrol Inspector to drive the Attorney General while he was in Montgomery. One night during the week, the Attorney General came to the command center around midnight, and a short time later I accompanied him to his car, but there was no driver. I saw a light about a block away that was an all night restaurant. I went there and found the driver eating. That night I requested Chamblee to select another driver for the Attorney General, which he did. Several years later and after I retired, I was selling raffle tickets at a retiree conference when a former officer came up to buy some tickets. During the transaction I introduced myself, and he said, "Oh, I know who you are." It was the driver that I had replaced.

On the last night of the demonstration, the marchers were camped a short distance from Montgomery. Chief Chamblee and I visited the camp. It had been raining and conditions there were deplorable, but Martin Luther King Jr., other leaders and the marchers all seemed to be in good spirits. The Border Patrol had provided protection for the marchers and there had been no incidents. I was most grateful for the manner in which they had conducted themselves. The marchers arrived at the Capital building around 2:00 p.m., and after several speeches, the march officially ended and the crowd dispersed. I took the Attorney General to the airport for his return flight to Washington. He told me to call him if there were any incidents, and he asked me to check with the FBI that evening. After returning to Montgomery, I told Chamblee to give the officers the rest of the day off. As I said earlier, there had been no incidents during the march, and I was very pleased with the performance of the Border Patrol Officers. A little later I received word that a lady from Detroit, Michigan who had been one of the marchers was shot and killed while she was driving back to Selma, Alabama. A car pulled along side hers and someone shot her. I called the Attorney

General and informed him of the murder. As requested by the Attorney General, I checked in with the FBI and I told them of the murder. They told me that had not heard of any other incidents. There were several agents in the office, and when I left I felt that I had been about as welcome as a skunk at a social function. The following day we all returned to our official stations.

Chapter Eleven
Seize of the Pentagon

In early October of 1967, it became known that "Peaceniks" from all over the United States were coming to Washington, D. C. to protest the Vietnam War, and that they were going to demonstrate at the Pentagon on October 21st and 22nd. On the morning of October 16th I received a call from Chief U. S. Marshall James McShane requesting that fifty Border patrol officers be detailed to Washington, D. C., to assist the Marshalls in providing security during the demonstration at the Pentagon. Arrangements were made for the detail, and the officers were instructed to arrive in Washington on Wednesday, October 18th, and to report to the local Chief Marshall, Luke Moore, at the U. S. Courthouse on Constitution Avenue at 7:00 p.m., where they would be briefed on their coming assignment. I attended the briefing, but I was not asked to participate in the operation. On Thursday they received an additional briefing by the Attorney General. Additionally, I was asked to have a radio base station installed in the Department of Justice building so the Attorney General could keep abreast of developments.

On Friday, October 20th, before I went to my office, I visited the radio base station at the Department of Justice to assure myself that there were no problems.

The Deputy Attorney General came in while I was there. He asked me if I was going to the Pentagon, and when I replied that I wasn't, he asked why. I told him that I had not been invited. He then said the Attorney General expects and wants you to be there. The Deputy was going to the Pentagon, so I rode with him in his chauffeured limousine. After arriving, I attended a briefing regarding plans that had been made to secure the Pentagon for the benefit of the Secretary of Defense Robert McNamara and the Attorney General Ramsey Clark. After the meeting Mr. Clark told me that I would be in charge of the enforcement operations, and if demonstrators committed an offense, I was to have them arrested, and they would be sent to a Federal Detention Facility some fifteen miles south of the Pentagon. There was a platoon of Marines in an "at ease" formation surrounding the Southwest entrance to the Pentagon. The protestors wanted to storm the building, and when they couldn't reach the entrance, they were extremely frustrated. It happened several times – a protestor would stand directly in front of a Marine with his face touching or almost touching the Marine's face and would then spit in his face; or the demonstrator would have a cigarette in his hand and burn the Marine's hand. When this happened, the Marine would step aside and an officer would pull the offender through the line and arrest him. I don't recall how many were arrested, but it was a large number. During the two days of the demonstration, it was common practice for the protestors to be resting or asleep under trailers and trucks. When it was time for the news, the TV crews would shout it's time for the news, let's start demonstrating. During the demonstration my long time friend and associate Charles Chamblee assisted me. We stayed at the Pentagon from Friday morning until Sunday morning when the demonstrators departed. The Border Patrol Officers did an exceptionally fine job and I was proud of the way that they had conducted themselves.

All of the Border Patrol Officers were requested to remain in Washington through Monday, October 23rd, to attend a meeting at 3:30 p.m. in the Great Hall of the Department of Justice. At the meeting the Attorney General thanked and commended them for their fine work at the Pentagon.

DEPUTY ATTORNEY GENERAL

WASHINGTON

October 26, 1967

Mr. Donald R. Coppock
Assistant Commissioner, Enforcement
Immigration and Naturalization Service
Rm. 677
119 D Street, N.E.
Washington, D. C.

Dear Don:

   We have come to expect a great deal from
the Border Patrol -- largely, I think, because
that is what we always get. The performance
of the Patrol at the Pentagon over the past
week-end was most certainly no exception.

   I heard nothing but praise for the calm
and professional manner in which your men went
about their assignments. With little rest,
and under constant strain, these men worked
long and skillfully. During the critical
period, the cars of the Patrol were the only
non-military means of transportation to or
from the reservation.

   I want you to know of my personal appreciation as well as the pleasure I take in looking
forward to future association with you.

   With best regards.

                    Sincerely,

                    Warren Christopher

Chapter Twelve
Martin Luther King, Jr. & His Assassination

This chapter relates to the late Martin Luther King, Jr. and events that led up to his death. In the 1960's, the FBI had a liaison officer who visited the Investigations and the Border Patrol Divisions of the Immigration Service on a regular basis. One day he came into my office and out-of-the blue stated that Martin Luther King Jr. was a philanderer, and during the time he was in Oslo, Norway to receive the Nobel Peace Prize he had affairs with different women. The statement really astounded me, but I had heard that J. Edgar Hoover, Director of the FBI, bitterly disliked Dr. King, and the liaison officer had probably been told to discredit him to the extent possible.

Dr. King was well known for his peaceful and nonviolent efforts to end segregation. In 1967 Dr. King and the Southern Christian Leadership Conference (SCLC) began discussions that would broaden their movement and address the true problems America faced. They planned to lead a march of several thousand of the nations poor and disenfranchised in Washington, D.C. to demand redress of their grievances and to demand jobs and incomes for them. It would become known as the

Poor Peoples March. In the mean time, there was a crippling strike of sanitation workers in Memphis, Tennessee. The issue, as explained to Dr. King, was the refusal of the City of Memphis to be fair and honest with its sanitation workers. Most of them were black. More than a thousand of them were on strike, and they were not about to make any concessions until their demands were met. The worker's demands were for better working conditions and better wages. The average wage was $1.80 per hour. The wages were so low that forty percent of the workers qualified for welfare and many worked second jobs. Almost two weeks later, while Dr. King was in New York giving a speech, Memphis police, using billy clubs and mace, attacked a small peaceful march of sanitation workers. This was the background that compelled Dr. King to alter his travel plans and head for Memphis. The board of directors did not endorse this decision. Their focus was on the planned Poor Peoples March in Washington, D.C. Dr. King believed otherwise. He didn't think that in good conscience he could turn his back on the black sanitation workers. Moreover, he concluded being there was consistent with the overall objectives of his campaign. Dr. King was supposed to lead another march that was scheduled for March 28th. Because his plane was late, Dr. King arrived in Memphis after the march had begun. He was quickly rushed by car to the front of the march. He immediately became aware that the march was not very well organized. The more than five thousand marchers were spread out helter-skelter across Beale Street. Chaos erupted, the police pummeled marchers, sixty-two marchers were seriously injured, and one young man died after being shot in the back. Dr. King was escorted away from the march, while six hundred police officers dispersed the marchers with tear gas and night sticks, arresting more than one hundred and fifty.

On the morning of April 1, 1968, Reverend King returned to Memphis to help organize another march to bring more attention to the sanitation worker's grievances. That night he gave a speech at the Clayton Temple Church. In spite of a violent thunderstorm, a crowd of two thousand was jammed into the church. It was to be Mr. King's last speech, and it is regarded as one of his most memorable ones. He was interrupted again and again by applause. His final words dwelt on his mortality, his close call with death, and then declared he was ready for whatever would be the outcome: *"Well, I don't know what will happen now. We've got some difficult days ahead, but it doesn't matter with me now. Because I've seen the mountaintop...I've seen the Promised Land. I may not get there with you. But I want you to know tonight, that we, as a people, will get to the Promised Land."* After the speech, the crowd was on it's feet shouting and applauding. Even the television crewmembers were applauding.

The next day, April 4, 1968, Dr. King was in a cheerful mood, lounging in his brother's room at the Lorraine Motel on Mulberry Street. That evening he was told that friends were there to take him to dinner. He went to his room to dress; then he and Reverend Jesse Jackson stepped out on the balcony. Reverend Jackson later stated that he thought he heard a firecracker, and when he looked at where Dr. King was standing, he wasn't there. He was lying on the balcony floor. He had been shot in the neck and killed.

I was asked to come to the Attorney General's office for a meeting the next day. I was told that there was a plan to have a march in Memphis, Tennessee on April 8th in honor of Dr. King, and that Mrs. King and her children were to lead the march. I was requested to provide Border Patrol officers to monitor the march to help ensure the marchers safety, and to provide a radio base station in the Federal Building so the Attorney General could stay informed of the proceedings. I also was asked to drive around the city and attempt to determine the mood of the people. To put it mildly, the colored citizens were extremely upset. I, along with another person whose name I don't recall, drove around Washington, and we determined that the citizenry was extremely upset. Cars with four and five colored males were a common sight cruising around the city, and they appeared to be in really foul moods. At times, I felt that we might be in danger. We returned to the Department of Justice and informed the Attorney General of the ugly mood of the people and suggested that a curfew be ordered. Soon after that, I accompanied the Attorney General to a meeting with the Mayor and the Chief of Police. The seriousness of the situation was discussed, and the mayor decided to order a curfew. Curfews were also mandated in many other cities. Many colored citizens in Washington ignored the ordered curfew. They broke out windows, looted stores and burned buildings, mostly in the colored sections of the city. It was a frightening night. When I went home at 3:00 a.m. the next morning, I had my service revolver lying on the seat beside me. Fires were burning in many, many locations.

On April 6th, I was specifically requested to assign a detail of twelve Border Patrol Officers and myself to Memphis, Tennessee. I was also asked to have our radio technician set up a radio base station on the 12th floor of the Federal Building, which was to be the command center while the officers monitored the march. In addition, I was to furnish nine handie-talkies, and the Border Patrol vehicles were to be unmarked. I departed for Memphis that afternoon, and the other officers were requested to arrive in Memphis before noon on the 7th of April. Upon their arrival, they were sworn in as Deputy United States Marshals, and on Monday, April 8th, the officers monitored the march, which ended late in the afternoon. It was a peaceful march and no incidents occurred.

On the evening of April 8th I was asked to move the operation to Atlanta, Georgia, with instructions for our officers to monitor the funeral services of Dr. King, and to also furnish radio communications. A base radio station was set up on the 5th floor of the Post Office Building, which was to be the command center, and an antenna was installed on the top of the building. The officers departed Memphis around 6:30 p.m., arriving in Atlanta at 5:30 a.m. My immediate supervisor, James F. Greene, detailed an additional fourteen officers to Atlanta. The officers monitored Dr. King's services at the Ebenezer Baptist Church and at Morehouse College.

Thousands attended the services and we were pleased that there were no incidents.

After the services were concluded, the Border Patrol Officers were exhausted, having worked over twenty-four hours with no sleep. I thanked them and told them they could get some sleep or return to their official stations. I personally thanked New Orleans Chief Patrol Inspector, Charles Chamblee, who was the officers' immediate supervisor. He was especially good at handling his subordinates, and he helped me in practically all of the civil disturbances in which the Border Patrol was involved. He was an exceptionally fine officer.

I have many remembrances relating to Dr. King and his work. I think what FBI Director J. Edgar Hoover said about Dr. King was a dastardly act, and he was completely out of line. I have no way of knowing whether Dr. King had affairs or trysts. But, I do know that what he did to help end segregation in a peaceful and non-violent manner was eventful, and that he will be long remembered for his fine work.

THE ATTORNEY GENERAL
WASHINGTON

April 16, 1968

Dear Don:

The resources of the Department of Justice were strained as never before by the tragic events of recent days. Our heavy and far-flung responsibilities demanded extraordinary services of you and others.

The services were rendered with clear commitment to our purpose; the responsibilities were met effectively.

My thanks will add little to your greatest reward -- the knowledge that your time, energy and ability helped your country meet a difficult challenge. Nonetheless, let me express my deep personal appreciation for your help.

Sincerely,

Ramsey Clark

Attorney General

Mr. Donald R. Coppock
Assistant Commissioner
Immigration & Naturalization
  Service
119 D Street, N. E.
Washington, D.C. 20536

Chapter Thirteen
Poor People's March on Washington

On February 27, 1968, I attended a meeting at the Department of Justice relating to the planned POOR PEOPLE'S MARCH ON WASHING-TON, D.C. that was organized by Martin Luther King, Jr. and the Southern Christian Leadership Conference. We were told that the demonstration was tentatively scheduled to start on April 15th, but the date was not firm. Around three thousand demonstrators were expected to attend, and Dr. King had men and women in fifteen different cities recruiting demonstrators. The length of the demonstration was unknown, but Dr. King had stated he expected it to exist until desired legislation was passed. I was told to plan on placing a base radio station in the Department of Justice Building, and to plan on furnishing Border Patrol Officers to monitor the demonstrators and to help keep the demonstration peaceful. The number of officers I was to provide would be decided at a later time. The Department of Justice must have thought the planned demonstration might have a detrimental effect on the operation of the government, such as closing down agencies and possible injury to government employees. Fred Vinson, Assistant Attorney General in charge of the Criminal Division and the point man for the operation, sent a sixteen-page letter of guidelines to government agencies that might be affected, and to all police departments in the District of Columbia. I was furnished a copy of the letter. Demonstrations were scheduled to be held at eight government buildings and memorials. Direct-line communications were established from the command center in the Department of Justice Building to the Secret Service, White House Police, Metropolitan Police, Capitol Police, Park Police, the General Services Administration, the Department of the Army and the U.S. Attorney's Office.

On May 12, 1968, thirty-eight Border Patrol officers reported for duty at the Department of Justice Building in Washington, D.C. After a briefing by Fred Vinson, they were sworn in as Deputy United States Marshals. On the morning of May 13th, the base radio station was activated in the command center, which was manned twenty-four hours a day for the duration of the demonstration. The Border Patrol's assignment was to monitor the perimeter of what was referred to as "tent city" where the demonstrators were assembled in West Potomac Park. Three radio equipped Border cars with two officers in each car were assigned to the operation 24/7. Two cars patrolled around the camp, and one unit patrolled the downtown area of Washington, D.C. Additionally, since it overlooked West Potomac Park, one officer was stationed on the top floor of the Washington Monument from 7:00 a.m. to 11:00 p.m., the hours the monument was open to the public. He was equipped with a handie-talkie in order to report any unusual developments. Assistant Attorney General Fred Vinson and his team met with leaders of the demonstration about ways to reduce violence by the marchers. The leaders of the demonstrators agreed to appoint reasonable members of the group to act as Rangers to help keep the members under control and to help reduce any violence that might be planned. The Rangers were generally effective and they helped keep a Border Patrol Officer from being attacked, which I will discuss later.

Although Martin Luther King, Jr. was assassinated prior to the Poor People's March, it was often referred to as the Martin Luther King Jr. March. On June 23rd, Patrol Inspector Bruce Plaskett was on duty at the observation windows atop the Washington Monument. He had laid his handie-talkie on the shelf while scanning tent city with his binoculars, but when he reached for his handie-talkie it was gone. Two men from Philadelphia who had taken it were starting to descend the stairs when Plaskett stopped and held them until the Park Police arrived and arrested them. The two men were charged with grand larceny. Also, in June, Border Patrol Inspector James Conley, while at his duty post on the north end of tent city by the reflecting pool, was requested by base radio to check on trouble that was occurring in the compound. Upon reaching the area at about 6:30 p.m., he reported to the command center that the troublemakers were outside the camp area throwing rocks and bottles at people passing by the area, and they seemed quite agitated and one citizen was injured. After the Rangers got the group back inside the compound and the trouble subsided, Patrol Inspector Conley, while returning to his duty post, was surrounded and accosted by about fifteen dissidents who tried to seize his handie-talkie. As this was happening, he told the group that he was a Federal officer and if they injured him they would be subject to a fine and jail time. While this was going on several camp Rangers arrived on the scene and dispersed the crowd.

On June 19th the group observed a SOLIDARITY DAY. It was presided over by Dr. Benjamin Mays, President Emeritus of Morehouse College. Dignitaries gave many speeches, and the Reverend Andrew Young, Executive Vice-President of the Southern Christian Leadership Conference, gave a solemn and rousing tribute to the late Martin Luther King Jr. He was their hero. A few days after the ceremony, the demonstration ended. The Department of Justice had become accustomed to the Border Patrol helping them enforce the recently enacted civil rights statutes during civil rights disturbances. As usual, the Border Patrol Officers, led by Chief Patrol Inspector Charles Chamblee, did a very competent and professional job during the Poor People's March for which I was most grateful.

Chapter Fourteen

Cesar Chavez and His Farm Workers Union

C esar Estrada Chavez was born March 31, 1927. He was a farm worker, labor leader and activist who co-founded the National Farm Workers Association, which later became known as the United Farm Workers Union. I mention this because he became so well known that his birthday became a holiday in a handful of states and a number of parks, libraries, schools and streets have been named in his honor. Additionally, in the year 2003, the U.S. Postal Service issued a thirty-seven cent stamp with his photograph in remembrance of him and his work. In 1942, Mr. Chavez graduated from the eighth grade. He could not attend high school because his father had been injured in an accident and he had to work to help support his family. He became known as what was called "a migrant farm worker". While his schooling was not the best, later in his life education became his passion. He was well read and the walls of his office in Delano, California were lined with hundreds of books ranging from philosophy, economics, cooperatives and unions, to biographies of Ghandi and the Kennedys. Through his life he became self-educated. He was the founder and the President of the United Farm Workers Union, and he devoted his efforts to organizing farm laborers in California and elsewhere, to get better wages and living standards for them. On September 8, 1965, Chavez initiated a strike of the grape workers in California who were asking for higher wages. The strike was to last for five years. Six months later, he headed the historic farm workers march from Delano to Sacramento, the Capital of California. While attempting to organize the farm workers, Chavez made numerous claims that the Border Patrol was trying to break the strike by permitting the growers to use illegal aliens. When he claimed that specific growers were employing illegal aliens, the Border Patrol would check their laborers to determine if any were illegal. Usually no illegal aliens were found. In 1969 Chavez, members of the United Farm Workers Union and many of his followers marched from Delano through the Coachella and Imperial Valleys to the border of Mexico to protest the grower's use of illegal aliens as replacement workers during the strike of his union members. Plea after plea was made nationwide for the public not to buy grapes. Accompanying Chavez and others on the march was the Reverend Ralph Abernathy, President of the Southern Christian Leadership Conference, and Senator Walter Mondale. Because of their presence, Chavez's repeated claim, that the Border Patrol was helping to break his strike by permitting growers to use illegal Mexican laborers, got national attention.

The AFL-CIO Union headquartered in Washington, D.C., with some thirteen million members, was trying to help Chavez with his organizing efforts, and it had its sights on possibly taking over the union. After the march was over, John J. Sweeney, President of the AFL-CIO Union, called the Attorney General and lodged a complaint that the Border Patrol was trying to help the growers break the strike by allowing them to use illegal aliens. The Attorney General called me and asked me to accompany him to a meeting with Mr. Sweeney. During the meeting, Mr. Sweeney stated emphatically that the Border Patrol was in bed with the growers and was allowing them to use illegal aliens. I told Mr. Sweeney that if he could tell me which growers were using illegal aliens, the Border Patrol would check their laborers that day or within a few days. He still claimed that we were helping the growers, and when I told him that his claim was not true, the Attorney General tapped me on the knee and said let it go. After the meeting, the Attorney General told me, *"We all know that union leaders lie."* During the meeting, Mr. Sweeney and the Attorney General agreed that the officers in the Livermore Border Patrol Sector and I would meet Cesar Chavez and his officials in Delano, California to hear their grievances the following week. I made arrangements for the meeting to start the following Tuesday. In the meantime, Mario Noto, Associate Commissioner, informed me that he was going to accompany me to the meeting. To this day I don't know whether he didn't trust me, or whether he was envious of my dealing with the Attorney General. The officers of the Livermore Sector, Mr. Noto and myself met the evening before the big meeting with Chavez and his officials. The officers were informed of the charges leveled against them and the reasons for their presence at the meeting. After I had explained this to the officers, Mr. Noto took the floor and, in a vicious and demeaning manner, berated the officers and the Border Patrol. His statements were unnecessary and uncalled for, as the sector officers had continually performed their duties in a most commendable manner. I could only assume that he was upset with me, envious of the Border Patrol, and wanted to demean the organization, and, as I have previously stated, he had never served in the Border Patrol. The Border Patrol's work was often used in budget hearings to obtain funds for the Immigration Service, but was forgotten after the funds were received.

The meeting with Mr. Chavez, his officials and organizers lasted the better part of two days. We sat there passively and listened to all kinds of verbal abuse and charges that we were trying to break his strike by permitting growers to use illegal aliens. I, of course, denied the charges, and I informed the group that if they knew where illegal aliens were employed they should tell us and we would check the laborers immediately. A vineyard near Delano was selected, and after the meeting, Mr. Chavez rode with me so that he could direct us to the vineyard. Mr. Chavez was affable and friendly during the trip. The laborers at the vineyard were checked, and no illegal aliens were found. An incident, which gave me a chuckle, occurred while the officers were checking the laborers. The owner of the vineyard asked Mr. Noto, who was in a business suit, if he was a Border Patrol officer. When he replied in the negative, the owner ordered him off his property. After the laborers were checked, the officers returned to their official stations. The charges from the union officials subsided, and matters returned to normal.

Chapter Fifteen
Increases of Illegal Entries and Answers to the Problem

The year 1968 was a banner year in my career. I was promoted to the position of Deputy Associate Commissioner for Enforcement, which was responsible for the operations of the Border Patrol and the Investigation Divisions of the Immigration Service. The Attorney General stated that he wanted me to have direct supervision of the Border Patrol, and as a result, the position of Assistant Commissioner Border Patrol was abolished. I'm sure that this distressed some of the higher echelon officials of the Immigration Service. Soon thereafter I was invited to the White House, where I met president Johnson and was given a tour of the White House by James Jones, assistant to the President and a former member of congress from Oklahoma. Additionally, in 1968 I received the Department of Justice DISTINGUISHED SERVICE AWARD. I don't want to leave the impression that I am boasting, far from it. The credit goes to all of the journeymen and supervisory officers who did the yeomen's work that made the Border Patrol, and eventually me, look good. They deserve all of the credit.

One day the Commissioner of the Immigration and

Naturalization Service, Raymond Farrell, called and asked me to come to his office. He apparently wanted to do something nice for me as he asked, *"Don, you have a daughter in Guam, don't you?"* I told him that my daughter Mary-Blue and her husband, John, were living in Guam, as he was a Lieutenant Commander in the Navy and was stationed there. Mr. Farrell then said, *"I think because of your new responsibilities, you should inspect the Investigation Divisions in Hawaii and Guam."* My wife Shirley accompanied me, and we had an interesting trip. While we were there, our second grandchild Donald William was born.

During the years from 1965 to 1973, in spite of bus lifts that were used to remove illegal Mexican aliens some 150 miles into the interior of Mexico to discourage their return to the United States, apprehensions increased from forty-five thousand to nearly three hundred and seventy thousand annually. The bus lifts were not as effective as the airlift, since they didn't take the illegals as far into the interior of Mexico, thereby making it more unprofitable for their illegal return to this country. The best, and really the only way to control the illegal entry of Mexican aliens, is to take the profit out of their illegal entry. This will be discussed in detail later. As I write this, the Congress has just passed legislation to build 700 miles of additional fencing along the Mexican border, which will cost billions of dollars, and when it is completed it will, in my opinion, only modestly help control the illegal entry of Mexican aliens. Laws making it a crime to knowingly employ illegal aliens have been on the books since 1970, but neither Republican or Democratic administrations have had the resolve to meaningfully enforce these laws.

I don't like to be critical, but President Bush, who has had worldly problems on his plate such as the World Trade Center bombings of September 11, 2001, and the Iraq War, has let his compassionate conservatism get out of hand relating to the illegal alien problem. He wanted to grant amnesty to the estimated twelve million illegal aliens in the United States, giving them preference over those who were patiently waiting in line to be admitted legally. This would have certainly rewarded them for their illegal entry. His views were completely out of step with views of the members of the House of Representatives and with those of the general public. The House of Representatives wanted to secure the border before any amnesty or guest worker program was considered. Although the President took an oath when he was sworn in that he would faithfully enforce the laws of the United States, the immigration laws must not have been included. He criticized the Minutemen, who were guarding locations along the border by calling them vigilantes, and he criticized the Border Patrol when they apprehended aliens who were employed, stating they should be apprehending criminals and terrorists. For goodness sake, it is the Border Patrol's mission and statutory authority to apprehend aliens who are in the United States illegally. The number of illegal aliens in the United States continues to increase, and meaningful steps must be taken to correct the situation. We simply cannot assimilate all of the poor and uneducated aliens coming here from Mexico and all over the world. The border states and many other states are suffering financially by the increase in costs of treating illegal aliens in emergency rooms; in hospitals; in welfare, including food stamps; the increase in costs in schools; and the increase in crime.

As this is being written, the unemployment figures in the United States are at four and a half percent, the lowest it has been in generations. Accordingly, it is evident that a guest worker program is needed. Legalizing those illegal aliens that are presently here is not the answer. To do this would cause thousands upon thousands of other aliens to come here to be included in the program. The Mexican government has long been known for it's corrupt practices. The country seems to have it's rich and it's very poor. There are relatively few in the middle class financially. The illegal entry of Mexico's poor into the United States has long been a safety valve that possibly has kept their poor from revolting. I would estimate that well over ninety-eight percent of the Mexican aliens that come here illegally come for economic reasons, and to improve their standard of living. The following few sentences describe the answer/solution to the decades long problem of the illegal entry of aliens across the Mexican border. Return adult male Mexican aliens to the interior of Mexico. It would take the profit out of their coming here, and they would stay home. Women and juvenile repeat offenders would be expelled at a location some fifteen to twenty miles from their homes. The answer to the problem is that simple.

A guest worker program is needed, and the Mexican government would welcome it, as they want work for their poor. The following described program is fair and it would help to solve the problem of what to do with the estimated twelve or more million illegal aliens that are presently in the United States, as many, if not most, of them would voluntarily return to Mexico to obtain a permit that would allow them to come here legally. A contract with Mexico must, and I repeat, must have a clause that permits the United States to remove apprehended aliens to the interior of Mexico. After such a program is activated, we need to have the authority to remove Mexican males to the interior of their country in order to take the profit out of their coming here illegally. Those negotiating a guest worker program with Mexico should insist that the migration center, where applicants gather to apply for permits to come to the United States legally, be at a location in the interior of Mexico, such as Chihuahua, Chih., Mexico, which is located about three hundred and fifty miles from the border. This would be beneficial to the applicants as it is centrally located, and it would be a benefit to the United States as those applicants who are denied permits would not be tempted to enter the United States illegally. Such a program would be more effective and not as expensive as a 700-mile fence along the border.

I recently read some statistics that urgently supports the need to solve the illegal alien problem. There are billions of impoverished people in the world. For the one million illegal aliens the United States has been absorbing each year, the number of indigent and impoverished people in third world countries increases between seventy and eighty million. We have empathy for them, but there is no way that we could absorb them. Read the following FBI statistics and you will probably be unhappy that our government is not doing more to correct the illegal alien problem we have in the United States.

- At the present time the State of California is building a new schoolhouse each and every day, and will into perpetuity if conditions don't change.
- Ninety-five percent of all warrants of arrest for murder in Los Angeles are for illegal aliens.
- Eighty-six percent of warrants for murder in Albuquerque are for illegal aliens.
- Twenty-nine percent (630,000) convicted illegal alien felons fill our state and federal prisons at a cost of $1.6 billion annually.
- Seventy-five percent of those on the most wanted list in Los Angeles, Phoenix and Albuquerque are for illegal aliens.
- Sixty-six percent of stopped/cited drivers in New Mexico have no license, no insurance and no registration. Of the sixty-six percent, ninety-eight percent are illegal aliens.
- In the year 2005, over 380,000 babies were born in the United States to illegal alien parents; those newborns became U. S. Citizens. Over sixty-six percent of all births in California are to illegal alien Mexican mothers on med-cal, whose births are paid by the taxpayers.

There are many more such statistics, but you get the picture from these figures.

An article written by F. Wooldridge, dated September 21, 2006, regarding diseased illegal aliens in the United

States is quite an eye opener. He stated that, as of last week, one hundred forty-six citizens in twenty-three states suffered from an E-Coli infection and one died. To bring this into focus, he further stated that twenty million illegal aliens crossed into the United States in the last twenty years without any kind of health screening. They work picking our food, washing our dishes in restaurants and, as is the norm in third world countries, rarely, if ever, wash their hands after using the toilet. Additionally, most of them suffer from functional illiteracy. They do not practice the personal hygiene or health habits that most Americans are accustomed to as a normal aspect of living. The author had recently taken a trip through the continental forty-eight states where he saw thousands of illegal aliens working in fields. In many fields there were no porta-potties, and he saw no hand-washing facilities. At a restaurant in Pennsylvania, several customers died because the work staff suffered with hepatitis infections. The Center for Disease Control stated they thought the source originated in Mexican fields irrigated with sewage water. Additionally, there were many outbreaks of multi drug resistant tuberculosis cases in Philadelphia, Atlanta, and near Cleveland during the past summer. We have imported at least sixteen thousand cases of Tuberculosis in the past five years. Before that, TB was virtually extinct in America. We've imported seven thousand cases of Leprosy in the past three years. For the first time ever, it is a serious situation in the United States. Have you read about it in the press or heard about it on any of the major television or radio networks? Not a chance! Sixty-two of our one hundred senators voted for SB 2611 that would assure our growth by one hundred million over the next thirty-four years. The increase would be mostly from third world countries. That ensures pockets of poverty and disease, already ravaging millions in those countries, to be transplanted into America.

It appears that the congress and the administration do not realize or understand the gravity of the illegal alien problem. They seem to think more of the Mexican-American vote and power, than what is best for our country and our way of life. Where are our statesmen who are supposed to be looking out for our country? The situation gets worse each year, and the more it is prolonged, the worse it gets. I explained earlier in this chapter how I think the problem should be addressed. The solution should be acceptable to Mexico, the Congress of the United States and to the caring public. The answer worked for me, and it will work for our country now.

Distinguished Service Award

Donald R. COPPOCK, Deputy Associate Commissioner (Domestic Control) was honored by the Department of Justice in December when he was presented with the Attorney General's DISTINGUISHED SERVICE AWARD at a ceremony in the Great Hall. The award is one of three newly established to recognize particularly noteworthy service by Department executives.

Mr. Coppock was cited for his qualities of leadership which have brought the Border Patrol to new heights of achievement, not only in meeting the escalating demands of its assigned mission but also in responding to extraordinary demands, under the most trying circumstances, made in connection with the enforcement of Federal law and court orders.

Accompanying the citation was a handsome walnut plaque showing the Department Seal in bronze, and a metal name plate.

A native Oklahoman, Mr. Coppock is a graduate of Northwestern State College in that State. He joined the Border Patrol in 1941 and served in every supervisory position in the Patrol prior to being named Deputy Chief of Border Patrol at the Central Office in 1957. In 1961, he was advanced to Asst. Commissioner for Enforcement, and was named Deputy Associate Commissioner in 1968.

Donald R. Coppock

ATTORNEY GENERAL'S
DISTINGUISHED SERVICE AWARD

PRESENTED TO

DONALD R. COPPOCK

IMMIGRATION AND NATURALIZATION SERVICE

WASHINGTON, D.C.
DECEMBER 18, 1968

Ramsey Clark
ATTORNEY GENERAL

Chapter Sixteen
Operation Intercept

The last major assignment during my tenure as Chief of the Border Patrol was called OPERATION INTERCEPT. In 1969, President Richard Nixon requested that a major effort be made to intercept the clandestine movement of marijuana, narcotics, dangerous drugs and contraband from Mexico into the United States by surface and by air. The Border Patrol was put in charge of the operation, and I was the point man. The operation was to be closely coordinated with the Customs Service. A Customs Agent was to be assigned to, or be immediately available, at each Border Patrol Sector Headquarters to assist the Chief Patrol Inspector in coordinating any intelligence received. An order was issued stating that no action will be taken by the Customs Service to apprehend violators between the Ports of Entry without knowledge and concurrence of the Chief Patrol Inspector of the area involved. Tactical intelligence/information received from any source, foreign or domestic, which required urgent attention, was to be forwarded immediately to the Chief Patrol Inspector responsible for the area. Each Chief was to relay all intelligence information received from Port Isabel to El Paso, to the command center in Houston, Texas. Intelligence information received from Tucson to Chula Vista, California was to be sent to the command center at the Immigration Regional Headquarters on Terminal Island, California. Additionally, the air detail Headquarters was located in Yuma, Arizona. All intelligence information was to be relayed there by telephone. Eighty Investigators and 157 Patrol Inspectors were detailed to Border Patrol stations located along the Mexican border to assist in enforcing the land operations.

The legal entry of airplanes coming from Mexico to the United States from 1964 to 1969 had doubled, so it was logical to assume that the smuggling of aliens and contraband by air had increased. Since a directive from the President brought about the operation, every effort was made to detect and prevent the illegal entry of contraband by land and by air. All FAA radar facilities near and along the Mexican border, as well as the radar facilities of the Laughlin, Laredo, Del Rio and Luke Air Force Bases were utilized, and a Patrol Inspector was assigned to each location so that all infractions detected could immediately be reported to the appropriate official in order for the nearest pursuit plane to be alerted. At areas along the border that could not be covered by the FAA and the Air Force facilities, portable radars were installed. The inspection of vehicular traffic entering the United States from Mexico was greatly intensified. As the Border Patrol did not have a sufficient number of planes fast enough to use for pursuit purposes, two Beach Barons were furnished by the FAA; two Cessna 310s were furnished by the Department of Defense; two Beach Barons were furnished by the Customs Service; and two Beach Barons were leased by the Border Patrol.

Pilots with multi-engine and instrument ratings were detailed to attend the Federal Aviation Administrative training facility in Oklahoma City from September 3rd to the 9th for up to date instructions in flying these aircraft. The operation began September 15th and ended September 30, 1969. The apprehension of illegal aliens entering from Mexico substantially increased, as did the seizure of marijuana along the land border. At the beginning of the operation a plane entered the United States from Mexico near Calexico, California. Radar detected the violation, and a pursuit plane from El Centro was alerted. The Border Patrol pilot followed the plane west to the Pacific Ocean near San Diego where it turned north. The suspect plane turned back into the United States near Bakersfield, where it landed with the Border Patrol plane in hot pursuit. When the pilot and Border Patrol officer encountered the suspect, they found the plane loaded with marijuana. There was considerable news in the papers, radio and television. The smugglers must have learned about the operation and stayed home, as this was the last and only planeload of marijuana detected during the operation.

Chapter Seventeen

Retirement and Work with the Impeachment Inquiry Committee Relating to President Nixon

On June 30, 1973, at the age of 62, I retired from my position as Deputy Associate Commissioner for Enforcement. It was a hard decision, but I figured that it was time to turn in my badge. Over the years I had enjoyed playing golf on weekends. After retirement, I played golf for several straight days, and I found that it wasn't so enjoyable playing every day, especially without my buddies. I had worked all of my life, and I was lost and unhappy. This will come as a shock to my Quaker relatives, but as I had nothing to do, I drank too much. After a while, I realized that drinking was not helping. It was difficult, but thank goodness I was able to give it up.

In December of 1973, my wife Shirley and I took a train trip to California to visit our daughter Mary-Blue and her husband John Ster. John, a Lieutenant Commander in the Navy, was attending the Naval Post Graduate School in Monterrey. While there, we visited San Francisco and the surrounding area, including the Giant

Sequoia Forrest. It was a sight to behold. We also attended the Bing Crosby Pebble Beach Golf Tournament, as it was then called. What a beautiful layout it was; you could look across the bay and see the city of Carmel. After returning to Oklahoma, I received a call from John Doar, former Assistant Attorney General for Civil Rights. Mr. Doar had been selected to head the Impeachment Committee looking into the impeachment of President Richard M. Nixon. He asked if I would be available to take the position of Public Information Officer for the committee. Of course, I was most anxious to go back to work. I didn't know if I was qualified for the position, but I readily accepted the offer. At the time, I told Mr. Doar that my sympathies were for Mr. Nixon. Mr. Doar then said that it was healthy to have diversity on the committee. Upon returning to our home in Maryland in January of 1974, I immediately went to work for the committee. One of the first calls I received was from the well-known columnist Robert Novak, who asked me the history of the impeachment process. When I was unable to answer his question adequately, he gave me a very hard time. Of course, I immediately began learning and informing myself on the subject. It was interesting to learn that the impeachment was first used in England in the 16th century. Their Parliament was the supreme authority, not a coordinate branch of government as in the United States. An official in England could be impeached because of his religion, party affiliation, or by other broad charges. This procedure continued through the 18th century. The framers of our constitution studied the British system, but decided that the impeachment process must be based on specific charges. They specifically limited the grounds for impeachment to: TREASON, BRIBERY OR OTHER HIGH CRIMES AND MISDEMEANORS.

The Impeachment Inquiry Committee staff was housed on the second floor of a building near the Capitol and the House of Representatives. I was told not to permit any television crews or reporters on the premises. The first person to ask for an interview was Theodore White, a well-known and respected author. I refused the interview and politely escorted him down to the first floor of the building. When I returned to my office, Mr. Doar asked me who the person was. When I told him, he replied that Mr. White was an exception to the rule. Mr. White was still in the building, and I spent an enjoyable hour talking with him. Later, a television crew showed up wanting an interview. I, of course, refused and politely escorted them from the premises. A while later, the honorable Peter Rodino, Chairman of the House Judiciary Committee gave them an interview. There were many more requests for interviews, but all were discreetly denied. Additionally, there were numerous groups that came to Washington who were for and against the impeachment of the President. It was my task to meet with them and listen to their pleas and views. About two weeks after the hearings began, the Administrative Officer for the Committee resigned and returned to his law practice in Baltimore. Instead of hiring another person, Mr. Doar asked me to take over his responsibilities. So, I wore two hats throughout the hearings.

I would usually arrive at work around 7:00 or 7:30

a.m. daily, and would normally be there until 10:00 p.m., if not later. I was constantly on the phone answering questions about the hearings, and after the hearing concluded I supervised the distribution to 5,000 locations of 43 books relating to the hearings. Sets of books were sent to libraries, law schools, journalism schools, universities, colleges and state bar associations.

Almost daily I would receive calls that required a legal answer. I would usually tell the caller that I would get back to them, if I didn't know the answer. I talked to different attorneys, and I would often not get a definitive answer. I finally found a lady attorney, a recent graduate of the Yale Law School, who would give me clear and concise answers to my questions. Her name was Hillary Rodham. I can still see her dressed in a red suit with her feet on her desk. She was real pleasant to deal with, and we became well acquainted. She asked if, after the hearings when I was on my way to Oklahoma, I might stop by and see her at the Rose Law Firm in Little Rock, Arkansas. She had a brilliant mind and was never too busy to help.

After months of hearings, there were three Articles of Impeachment lodged against the President by the House of Representatives. Following here is a brief summary of the articles:

Article I: On June 17, 1972, agents of the Committee to Re-elect the President committed unlawful entry of the headquarters of the Democratic National Committee in Washington, D.C. for the purpose of securing political intelligence. Subsequent thereto Richard M. Nixon, using the power of his high office, engaged personally and through his subordinates, in a course of conduct to delay, impede, and obstruct the investigation of such unlawful entry, to cover up, conceal and protect those responsible for the break-in. There were many other specific charges, but they all were related to the botched burglary.

Article II: The President, acting personally and through his subordinates and agents, endeavored to obtain from the Internal Revenue Service, in violation of the constitutional rights of citizens, confidential information contained in income tax returns for purposes not authorized by law, and to cause, in violation of the constitutional rights of citizens, income tax audits or other income tax investigations to be initiated or conducted in a discriminatory manner. This article also contained several specific instances where the President had tried to use the IRS, the FBI and the CIA in violation of the constitution.

Article III: The President in his conduct of the office of President of the United States and, to the best of his ability, to preserve, protect and defend the Constitution of the United States and in violation of his constitutional duty to take care that the laws be faithfully executed, has failed without lawful cause or excuse to produce papers and things as directed by duly authorized subpoenas issued by the Committee on the Judiciary of the House of Representative on April 11, 1974; May 15, 1974; May 30, 1974; and June 24, 1974; and willfully disobeyed such subpoenas. The subpoenaed papers and things were deemed necessary by the Committee in order to resolve by direct evidence fundamental, factual question relating to Presidential direction, knowledge or approval of actions demonstrated by other evidence to be substantial grounds for impeachment of the President. In refusing to produce these papers and things, Richard M. Nixon, substituting his judgment as to what materials were necessary for the inquiry, interposed the powers of the President against lawful subpoenas of the House of Representatives, thereby assuming to himself functions and judgments necessary to the exercise of the sole power of impeachment vested by the Constitution in the House of Representatives.

It was discovered during the hearings that President Nixon had his conversations in the Oval Office tape-recorded. The House of Representatives' efforts to subpoena the tapes were mostly ignored, claiming Presidential privilege. The issue went to the courts, which ordered the President to surrender the tapes or copies thereof. They were sent to the House of Representative and then to the Impeachment Inquiry Committee. I was placed in charge of the tapes, and I was informed that I was to permit only those who needed to know to listen to them. The tapes were scratchy and hard to understand, but they revealed one very important fact: that President Nixon had participated in and ordered the cover up of the botched burglary of the Democratic National Committee Headquarters. That was the fatal fact that led to the President's resignation.

When Mr. Nixon was re-elected to his second term, he was very popular, and he won by a large margin. The charges in the first Article of Impeachment were the primary reasons for his downfall. If he had not tried to protect and defend the officials who were responsible for the break-in and had fired them, I think he would not have been impeached, and that his popularity would have soared.

President Nixon, seeing the handwriting on the wall, resigned his position as President of the United States at noon on August 8, 1974; before the Senate held his trial. After the President's resignation, the attorneys on the Inquiry Committee left and returned to their homes. John Doar, who headed the Inquiry Committee, informed me that he was taking a two week vacation to visit his childhood home in Wisconsin, and he told me that I was to be in charge while he was gone. Janet Howard, my assistant, was well connected politically, and she was a very competent administrator. We were kept busy answering telephone calls and written inquiries. There were 10 to 12 stenographers still working, and they were kept busy typing letters, etc. After a few days, I realized that the stenos were reliable in the morning, but in the afternoon most of them were useless. There was a restaurant in the building where the girls ate. The place served liquor, and most of them got crocked during the noon hour and were not able to function reliably during the afternoons. I discussed the matter with Janet Howard, and I fired those that were not doing their jobs. Looking back, I suppose that I was somewhat presumptuous. Everything went well until Mr. Doar returned. When he heard that I had terminated the girls' employment, he called a meeting of the staff and he gave me holy hell for what I had done. We were still friends, as I later visited him in his law office in New York, and we stayed in touch for years. In spite of his unkindly remarks, to this day I think that I did the right thing.

Chapter Eighteen
Work with the Legal Services Corporation

After the Impeachment Inquiry Committee's work was completed, I returned to Oklahoma to work on a house that I had bought. While there, I received a call from Louis Oberdorfer, former Assistant Attorney General for the Tax Division. He explained to me that the Congress had passed the Legal Services Act of 1974, thus creating the Legal Services Corporation (LSC), a quasi-government organization whose mission was to furnish high quality legal assistance to those who were unable to afford adequate legal counsel. This work had previously been the responsibility of the Office of Equal Opportunity Legal Services Program. He then said that he had been selected to handle the transition, and he asked if I would be available to help. Even though he thought the work would last about 30 days, I was most happy to get back to work again. The transition team was temporarily housed in offices on K Street in Washington, D.C. My first assignment was to find suitable office space for the new organization. After looking at numerous prospective locations, most of which were not suitable, I found space in the 10-story Woodward Building. The owners agreed to lease us a couple of floors at a reasonable price. It was centrally located and just a block from K Street. Mr. Oberdorfer approved of the location and arrangements were made to make the move over a weekend. In 1975, President Ford appointed the first Board of Directors, and Roger Crampton, Dean of the Cornell University Law School, was selected as Chairman of the Board. In 1977, the Legal Services Corporation Act was re-authorized, which provided LSC with greater flexibility to fund support activities. The Carter administration appointed new members to the LSC Board, including former University of Arkansas law professor and member of the Rose Law Firm in Little Rock, Hillary Rodham, who later married Bill Clinton. In 1978, her fellow Board members elected Hillary LSC Chairwoman.

After the move to the Legal Services Corporation's permanent location, I was selected (or I inherited the job) as the Corporation's Administrative Officer. My work with the organization, instead of lasting only 30 days, lasted for five years. I did all the purchasing for the organization, and I wrote their administrative manual. After a couple of years, a Chief Administrator was hired. He was an affable and capable administrator, but I was astonished to learn that he was a homosexual. I had met his wife, but it wasn't long before they were divorced. I and several other LSC employees were invited to his house for a party, and during the evening his male companion came out of their bedroom. I was kept busy during the remaining years of my tenure with a myriad of assignments.

In my work I was conscious of the need to keep

administrative costs low so that adequate funds would be available for the organization to help and represent the poor. This apparently was not a priority for the corporation, as many of the attorneys, when traveling would go first class, and one attorney, after moving to Miami, Florida, traveled there occasionally on weekends at government expense. I wrote Hillary Rodham, Chairman of the LSC Board of Directors about the situation, and I received a non-responsive reply. As I write this in early 2007, almost everyone thinks that Mrs. Clinton will be a strong candidate for President of the United States in 2008.

I recently received a copy of the Legal Services' Magazine, which was titled "30th Anniversary Special Edition", stating we're proud of what happens here. The magazine's feature article was a story by Legal Services' first Chairman of the Board of Directors, Roger Crampton, entitled "A Reflection of a Vibrant Start". He wrote a concise history of the corporation, remembering past events, past presidents of the corporation, and he especially commented on the work of Louis Oberdorfer, commending him as a public spirited Washington attorney who, on a sabbatical from his law firm, agreed to provide executive leadership during the transition of the corporation as part of a government agency to a quasi-government corporation. Attorney David Tatel was Mr. Oberdorfer's assistant, and as this is being written, both are on the Federal bench. Mr. Oberdorfer is a Senior District Judge and Mr. Tatel is a Circuit Court Judge. Over the years, I worked with and for Mr. Oberdorfer. He was a genial and competent leader, and we have stayed in touch over the years. The article also commented that Donald Coppock, former head of the Immigration and Naturalization Service Border Patrol, was ingenious in meeting LSC's infrastructure and equipment needs.

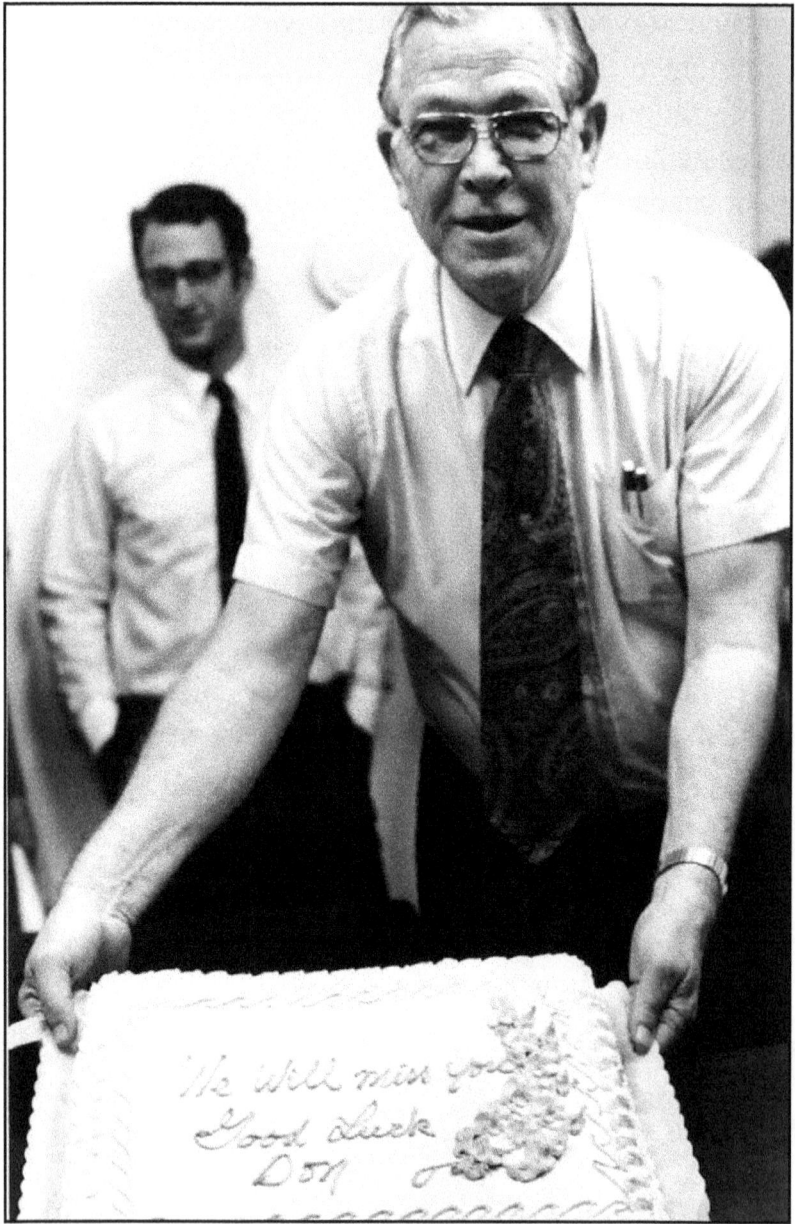

Departing the Legal Services Corporation in 1980 after five years of consulting work.

Chapter Nineteen
Life after Retirement

As I write this, in January of 2007, President Ford's services were being held at the National Cathedral in Washington, D.C. I couldn't help but shed a few tears, thinking how we honor our leaders and what a great country we are privileged to live in. I never had the pleasure of meeting Mr. Ford, but from what I have read and heard, he was a down to earth, nice, competent and genial person.

A few years after I retired from the Border Patrol, Gordon MacDonald, who was formerly on my staff, told me that he would like to organize a Border Patrol retirement organization. We met in downtown Washington, D.C. on numerous occasions to discuss what kind of organization we wanted and what was needed to achieve our goal. I want to make it clear that this was Gordon's idea and it was a good one. In October of 1978, 34 retired Border Patrol Officers and their wives met in Denver, Colorado to develop our new organization. Mr. MacDonald split us into groups, each with specific assignments. I headed one group and during our discussions I needed information from another group, so I asked former Chief Patrol Inspector Jeff Fell to please get the information from the group. He got up and, as he was leaving, he turned and said, *"Don,*

I don't work for you any more." I did not reply, and he went ahead and got the information that was needed. I told this story to my long time friend Bob Stewart, and he really had a good laugh about it and enjoyed relating the story to others. On October 25th, the last day of our meetings, the bylaws were adopted, and it was decided that the retirees would meet annually to fraternize and renew old acquaintances. Some wanted the organization to be active politically, but it was decided that it was to be fraternal only otherwise it could be divisive. Additionally, there were many suggestions as to what to call the new organization. It was suggested that it be called the FRATERNAL ORDER OF RETIRED BORDER PATROL OFFICERS (FORBPO). A vote was taken and the name was adopted. A Board of Directors was selected, and Jim Kelly, former Chief Patrol Inspector of the Tucson Sector, was named the first Chairman of the Board. He was an amiable, capable and all around nice person. We also decided to hold our first conference in Tucson in the spring of 1979.

During my tenure as Chief of the Border Patrol, I had dreams of a museum that would preserve the history of the Border Patrol. At the time, it was an impossible dream, as there was no way to raise funds for such a project. So, I did the next best thing. Over the years, the Border Patrol sponsored and funded individual and team pistol shooters that won numerous national, individual and team championships. Even though the government furnished the ammunition and paid entry fees, etc., individual trophies won were kept by the person who won them. I attempted to get as many individual and team trophies as possible sent to the Border Patrol Academy in Port Isabel, Texas. It was a nice display, and it was an inspiration to trainees attending the academy, but it in no way preserved the history of the Border Patrol.

As I said, the first FORBPO conference was held in Tucson in the spring of 1979. It was a success and the beginning of a very rewarding tradition. At that meeting I told Chairman Jim Kelly that our new organization should sponsor a worthwhile project. When he asked me if I had any suggestions, I told him that it would be difficult to accomplish, but the creation of a Border Patrol Museum would be a very worthwhile endeavor. Mr. Kelly then asked me to look into the feasibility of the idea and report back to the Board of Directors at our next conference, which was to be held in Las Vegas, Nevada. During the year I talked to an acquaintance who had previous experience in fund raising. He was not very encouraging when he told me that I would find that only about 8% of our membership would support the museum financially. In spite of his observation, I felt that our organization's members would do much better.

In 1980 at the conference in Las Vegas, I met with the Board of Directors and told them that raising funds for a museum would be difficult, but I thought we should move forward with the project. Sadly, the board took no action on the matter, and I found that I had many, many critics. The issue languished until the competent and well-respected Walt Edwards became Chairman of the Board. He persuaded the board to poll the membership about the issue. A vote was taken, and the members voted 320 to 11 in favor of going forward with the project. After the vote, I visited the National Association of Museums' Headquarters in Washington, regarding how to go about getting the museum designated as a non-profit organization. I was told that one of the best attorneys in the country, who specialized in helping non-profit organizations, was Carl Ryan, and that he resided in El Paso, Texas. It was a serendipity that at this time Roger "Buck" Brandemuehl was Chief of the Border Patrol. He was, and still is, a devoted and inspiring supporter of our museum. I asked Mr. Brandemuehl if I could use his office for a meeting on a Saturday. I met with the late Bob Stewart and the son of former Chief Patrol Inspector Charles Kirk. I can't positively recall his name, but I think it was Charles, Jr. We wrote the STATEMENT OF PURPOSE for our proposed museum, and during the meeting, Mr. Brandemuehl arrived and participated in our discussions. Charles Jr. worked for FEMA and was an intelligent and astute person. The members of his car pool called him their ombudsman.

Soon after this meeting, I traveled to El Paso and met with the late John Sanchez, Sue Turner and Henry McCormick. I mention their names since they were strong supporters of the museum, and they could be depended on to do what was needed at the local level. We decided to name our new organization the BORDER PATROL MUSEUM AND MEMORIAL LIBRARY FOUNDATION. In addition to preserving the patrol's history, we thought it would be advantageous to provide an in depth history of the Border Patrol, so students and scholars would have a place where they could research the history of the Border Patrol. The group was also told to try and find a location that would be suitable to house the museum.

After returning to my home in Maryland, I wrote approximately 50 grant proposals in an attempt to raise funds for the museum, but it was an uphill battle. We received a few thousand dollars, and I could understand why I wasn't more successful. Corporations and foundations with a choice between making a grant to the Border Patrol Museum and, for example, the Boy Scouts would be a "no brainier". They would usually choose the Boy Scouts. We were able to get a few donations from the members of FORBPO, but raising funds was a difficult challenge.

John Sanchez, who had been selected to head the trustees in El Paso, informed me that they had not been able to find a suitable location for the museum. I had a friend in Yuma, Arizona who I had worked with when I was a trainee at the Strauss, New Mexico horse station. He had joined the Army during World War II, and after the war ended, instead of re-entering the Border Patrol, he chose to return to Yuma, and at that time he was President of the three Valley National Banks there. I called Mr. Young and explained to him that we were looking for a location to house our museum. He told me that he was almost certain that the Mayor, the City Counsel and the Chamber of Commerce would be interested, and that he would look into the matter and get back in touch with me. He called back and reported that the city fathers would be delighted to have the museum in Yuma, and that they had a building that might be suitable. I, along with a few other trustees, met with Mr. Young and the city fathers in Yuma. They were enthusiastic about the possibility of us locating the museum in their city. When the meeting was over, we examined the building they had offered us, and we found that it would cost in the neighborhood of $100,000 to make it suitable for our needs. We had to turn down their offer, as we didn't have that kind of money. We weren't too disappointed though, since we all thought that the museum should be located in El Paso, as that was where the first Border Patrol Training School was held, and El Paso was centrally located along the Mexican border.

After making the judgment that the museum would be located in El Paso, we contacted attorney Carl Ryan and asked him to have our foundation incorporated in the State of Texas, and that he also get it designated as a non-profit organization under the Internal Revenue Code.

Suitable space for our museum was finally found in the basement of the Cortez Building in downtown El Paso. Raising funds to get started was difficult, but through a series of grants, donations and proceeds from our annual raffle, we were able to open the museum in 1985. A surprisingly large crowd attended, and the opening was a huge success. Several city dignitaries attended, as well as the local Chief of the Border Patrol and Buck Brandemuehl, the National Chief of the Border Patrol. The curator had done a great job in displaying the many artifacts that had been donated, and the museum was really quite attractive. It was soon discovered that the space was too small, but we had no other alternative. In 1990 our lease was terminated, and the Board of Trustees, after being unable to find a suitable location for the museum, voted to store the artifacts until we could construct a building of our own. Those were dark days for the museum, as it was almost impossible to raise funds. I even talked to our attorney, Carl Ryan, about dissolving the organization. His reply was to hang in there, as conditions might change. And, conditions did change. I felt like it was divine intervention. A former Border Patrol Officer named Jack Price had served in World War II, and upon his return to the United States, took advantage of the GI Bill and became a lawyer. Subsequently, he practiced law in Los Angeles, California. This is the story as he related it to me. One day he got a call from a retired doctor, who asked Mr. Price to come to his house and prepare a will for him. Jack asked him to come to his office, but the doctor insisted that Jack come to his home. Jack agreed, and accordingly, he and his secretary went to the doctor's house, where they sat around the kitchen table to prepare the will. The doctor stated that he had no heirs, and he asked Jack if he could leave his estate to him. Jack replied that it wouldn't be ethical. After more discussion, Jack suggested that he leave his estate to the Anthony L. Oneto American Legion Post. The post was named after a Border Patrol Officer who was killed in the line of duty, and the membership was restricted to active and retired Immigration and Border Patrol Officers. The doctor agreed, and Mr. Price's law firm prepared the will as requested.

Several months later, Mr. Price received a call from the District Attorney, who asked him if he was the Attorney of Record for the doctor. When he replied that he was, he was told that the doctor was in the morgue, and that he had been there for about 30 days. Jack then made arrangements for a funeral and burial of the doctor. A few days later Jack, his secretary and a few retired Border Patrol Officers went to the doctor's house to evaluate the estate. They started finding bundles of $100 bills in drawers and other locations in the house. They went to his garage where the doctor's old Cadillac was parked, but they had no keys to the car. So, they pried open the glove compartment and the trunk where they found more bundles of $100 bills. When the estate was settled, the American Legion Post was awarded $750,000.

John Sanchez, President of the Trustees in El Paso, learned that the city had land on Transmountain Road in North El Paso that had been set aside for museums and similar organizations. Mr. Sanchez approached the mayor and asked if we could obtain land there for our museum. He stated that we would need to get the approval of the city counsel. The counsel requested that we appear before their body and present our plans. Subsequently, many of the museum trustees appeared before the city counsel, and each spoke on behalf of the need for the land. We were strongly opposed by supporters of the Wilderness Museum, which was situated next to the land that we were interested in obtaining. They believed that we would destroy their nature trails, and that we would be a distraction from their museum. It was discovered that we would disturb only one trail, and the city counsel, after hearing of our plans, gave us a long term lease for two acres of land at $1 per year. Now all we had to do was to come up with the money to construct a suitable building.

Through a series of grants, donations, the selling of bricks with donor's names engraved on them, and a donation of $50,000 by the Anthony L. Oneto American Legion Post in 1989, we were able to raise approximately $185,000 by April of 1991. Trustee Sue Turner informed the Board of Trustees that she was acquainted with a well-known contractor who attended her church. His name was J. L. Reid, and he was President of the Westar Construction Group. A while later, members of the Board of Trustees met with Mr. Reid and his associates, and we were impressed by his resume and accomplishments. We explained our needs and requested that his firm furnish us with an architectural sketch of a 10,000 square foot structure, along with an estimated cost of a turnkey building. (See Photo) Later, Westar provided us with a proposal and contract, stating that the building would cost $500,000. After considering their proposal and after getting the approval of our sponsoring organization's Board of Directors of FORBPO, we signed the contract. Soon thereafter, the Anthony L. Oneto American Legion Post donated $150,000 more to help in funding a building for our museum. Their only request was that we provide a room to honor those who had lost their lives in the line of duty. Of course, we were more than happy to do that. We had space partitioned that we named the Anthony L. Oneto Memorial Room. The post donated additional funds for plaques and tablets that named and honored those who had given

*Top: A drawing of the U.S. Border Patrol Museum. Below: The
completed building.*

*Photo of the founders of the Fraternal Order of Retired Border
Patrol Officers, taken in Denver, Colorado, in 1978.*

their lives for their country. Through another series of grants, donations and raffles, we were able to pay for the entire cost of the building when it was completed. We moved our artifacts into our new 10,300 square foot building and in February of 1994 our new museum was opened. Several hundred dignitaries, officers and former officers and their families from all over the country attended the dedication ceremony. As I write this, we have been in our new building 13 years. The museum continues to grow and is getting better every year, thanks to the hundreds of volunteers and supporters who are building a legacy that will be appreciated and enjoyed by generations to come.

Over the years we have been fortunate to have such creative and dedicated people running the day-to-day operations of the museum, like Brenda Tisdale, the curator, and Kristi Rasura, the museum gift shop manager. I also want to mention and commend Gene Wood, a former Chief Patrol Inspector and President of the local Board of Governors for several years, who did an outstanding job overseeing the daily operations of the museum.

In 1998, after serving for 20 years as Chairman of the Board of Trustees, I resigned and turned over the gavel to my respected and capable deputy, Roger "Buck" Brandemuehl. I have remained on the Board and I still help support the museum, since I consider it a national treasure. To this day, I am thankful that our attorney, Carl Ryan, told me during the dark days not to dissolve the Museum Foundation, but to hang in there as conditions might change. He was so right!

In 1994, the same year the museum was reopened, we sold our house in Maryland and moved back to Cherokee, Oklahoma where I was born and raised. I farmed and ran cattle for a few years, but as I grew older, I had to give it up and rented out my farms. The only farming I do now is to mow around the farm buildings and a cemetery that my paternal grandfather helped to establish in 1894. I try to keep one farm stocked with quail, as I enjoy watching them.

I don't like to toot my own horn, but an incident occurred at our FORBPO conference in Phoenix, Arizona in 2006 that, to me, was very rewarding and made me feel that I had done something right during my career. After the closing banquet was over, a retired officer walked up to me, shook my hand and said, *"Mr. Coppock, I want to tell you that it was a pleasure working for you over the years, and that you were always a gentleman."* I thanked him, but I was so taken aback by the nice compliment, that I failed to ask him his name. If he reads this, I hope he will give me a call.

As I write this in early 2008 and near the end of my book the Congress has not passed legislation that would solve the illegal alien problem. It is a complex problem but it can be solved. Author and commentary Lou Dobbs stated in a late book that he wrote that our country's most serious problem was the terrorist threat closely followed by the illegal alien problem and I certainly agree. Our country cannot absorb the millions and millions of the world's poor and uneducated that would like to come to the United States. So, it is imperative that the congress acts properly to solve this most urgent problem.

It seems that the Democrats don't want to solve the problem because they want the Latino vote and the Republicans don't want to solve it because they want the cheap labor. Our country has serious problems such as the war and our enormous debt. If the illegal alien problem isn't solved conditions will only get much worse. President John Kennedy stated during his tenure as President: *"LETS NOT SEEK THE REPUBLICAN ANSWER OR THE DEMOCRATIC ANSWER BUT THE RIGHT ANSWER."* Lets hope the Congress will follow the President's advice.

In view of the Federal governments failure to solve the illegal alien problem, some states are passing legislation that would resolve the problem in their states. Last year the State of Oklahoma passed meaningful illegal alien legislation and it is working. Shortly after the legislation went into effect I received a call from a friend in the Dallas, Texas area who told me that the Dallas Morning News had a story titled: TEXAS IS BEING INVADED BY ILLEGAL ALIENS FROM OKLAHOMA. I'm sure the same happened in other border states. The legislation has saved the state millions of dollars and the legislation is being studied by other states.

Reflecting back on my long career in the Border Patrol, I am most appreciative of the camaraderie, professionalism and esprit-de-corps of the officers I worked with. It was a challenging, interesting, and rewarding journey. And as the song goes, "I'D LIKE TO DO IT AGAIN."

Sources

When I would return from a detail helping the Department of Justice enforce the Civil Rights statutes or other details in which the Border Patrol was involved, I would dictate a letter for my superiors and a copy for my personal file. These files provided me with the data and dates that were needed to write this book. Many of the stories were recalled by memory and other statistics were found on the Internet and other publications. Many of the events relating to my paternal grandparents, Alvin and Laura Coppock were taken from a book titled "The Life and Times of Alvin and Laura Coppock" written by my cousin, Sheldon Jackson.

Above, Don and Shirley. Right, Don in U.S. Border Patrol uniform.